W9-BVN-365

ideas for great
wall systems

By Scott Atkinson and
the Editors of Sunset Books

Menlo Park, California

Sunset Books

vice president, general manager:
Richard A. Smeby

vice president, editorial director:
Bob Doyle

production director:
Lory Day

director of operations:
Rosann Sutherland

retail sales development manager:
Linda Barker

executive editor:
Bridget Biscotti Bradley

art director:
Vasken Guiragossian

special sales:
Brad Moses

Staff for this book:

developmental editor:
Linda J. Selden

copy editor/indexer:
Barbara J. Braasch

photo director/stylist:
JoAnn Masaoka Van Atta

art director/page layout:
Kathy Avanzino Barone

illustrator:
Bill Oetinger

principal photographer:
Jamie Hadley

prepress coordinator:
Danielle Javier

proofreader:
Mary Roybal

Solutions for storage stress

Stow, stack, file, pile, and more with this new Sunset book as your guide. From shelves to cabinets to smooth-gliding TV carts, today's wall systems can help you solve a myriad of organization and display problems. What's your particular storage ill? You're sure to find a suitable remedy on the following pages.

Many retailers, design professionals, and homeowners shared their knowledge with us or allowed us to photograph their products and creations. We'd especially like to thank Eurodesign Ltd. of Los Altos, CA; Galvins Workspace Furniture of Redwood City, CA; Häfele America Company of San Francisco; Southern Lumber Company of San Jose, CA; Ikea of Emeryville, CA; and Organized Living of San Mateo, CA.

Individual credits for design and photography are listed on pages 126–127.

9 8 7 6 5 4 3 2 1
First printing June 2004
Copyright © 2004, Sunset Publishing Corporation,
Menlo Park, CA 94025. Second edition. All rights reserved, including
the right of reproduction in whole or in part in any form.

ISBN 0-376-01721-X
Library of Congress Control Number: 2003111885
Printed in the United States of America.

For additional copies of Ideas for Great Wall Systems or any other
Sunset book, call 1-800-526-5111 or visit us at www.sunset.com.

Cover main image: Scott Johnson, architect; photography by Tim Street-Porter.
Top left: photography by Brian Vanden Brink. Top middle: photography by
Jamie Hadley. Top right: photography by Thomas J. Story. Cover design by
Vasken Guiragossian.

contents

get organized!

BOOKS, TVS, COMPUTERS, compact discs, collectibles, sports gear—the piles of "stuff" that most people manage to accumulate over the years are staggering. Yet few homes provide enough space to stow all these goods in an orderly way.

When you can't stack your audio gear any higher, when your favorite collection is languishing in boxes in the basement, and when you can't wedge one more book onto your shelves, it's time to think about how to make better use of your present storage space or how to add to it without having to remodel your home or move to a new one.

One way to create a lasting solution to your organization and storage needs is to bring wall systems into the picture. What, you might ask, *is* a wall system? For an overview, see pages 8–9. A workable wall system can be as simple as an open shelf or as high-tech as a custom home-theater unit with drawers, doors, dividers, pullouts, and built-in speakers and lighting. Wall systems can stand alone or be built into a wall and finished to match the surroundings. They can hide messy storage items, showcase a prized collection, or perform both roles at once.

Deciding that you need a wall system is just the beginning. The next step is to evaluate your options. What items in your home need better organization? Where is the best place to put them? What approach works best? The first chapter of this book, "A Planning Primer," will guide you through the basics.

As you narrow down your choices, turn to the photos in the second chapter, "Great Wall Systems," for inspiration and ideas. You'll probably discover solutions you never thought of before.

Finally, you'll be ready to focus on the exact unit that's right for you. The third chapter, "A Shopper's Guide," will familiarize you with the myriad choices in shelves, cabinets, storage furnishings, and accessories on the market today.

In no time at all, you'll be enjoying the ease and convenience of a clutter-free home with a place for everything and everything in its place. Hopefully you've left some room for the *next* collection!

A PLANNING PRIMER

READY TO JUMP IN? In the second chapter, "Great Wall Systems," you'll see photo after photo of open shelves; bold, multiuse storage walls; freestanding furniture pieces; and the latest in media glamour and gizmos. BUT FIRST THINGS FIRST: This chapter will help you identify your basic needs and explore your options in styles and materials of both freestanding furniture pieces and seamless, custom built-ins. Then it's time for some basic engineering—important details on shelf spans; shelf connections; sizes for books, CDs, and other media accessories; and ergonomic heights and depths. We'll also travel through the latest options in entertainment centers and home theater hookups. FINALLY, WE TAKE A ROOM-BY-ROOM tour, outlining ways you can get wall systems and shelves to work for you in almost any situation. For a more in-depth look at specific components and hardware choices, turn to "A Shopper's Guide," beginning on page 87.

what is a wall system?

THE TERM *"wall system" is actually a catchall phrase that covers a broad sweep of furnishings used for display, organization, and storage. Wall systems range from simple open shelves to large component systems that include cabinets with doors, adjustable shelves, stacks of drawers, clothes rods, a desk, and even a drop-down bed. Traditional furniture pieces like armoires, hutches, and highboys may also fill the bill. These wall systems can go in virtually any room of the house and are used to store just about any household item.*

Shelves and boxes

Take a second to study the drawing on the facing page. You'll see horizontal shelves, vertical supports, drawer boxes, cabinet boxes, and doors that cover them. When it comes to wall systems, it all boils down to a matter of verticals, horizontals, and sometimes added boxes.

At its simplest, a wall system is a series of horizontal shelves hung on an open wall. Vertical sides or "uprights" support shelves inside a frame, like a shelving unit; shelves may be fixed or movable.

A bookcase is a frame that formalizes the relationship of both horizontals and verticals—in this example, a top, a bottom, and two sides. It often includes a back to keep the other elements firm and complete the box. A cabinet adds a door atop this open box. Drawers slide inside the box frame, too; think of them as "boxes within a box."

Bridge two boxes and you have a desk. Stack three tall boxes side-by-side and you have a media center. More elaborate systems add accessories such as hooks, sliding shelves, towers, racks, and other organizers.

Modularity is key

One feature characteristic of many wall systems is modularity. Components and accessories are often sized so that they can be interchanged and reconfigured as your needs change. Shelves can be raised or lowered, drawers refitted, and cabinet boxes stacked or ganged side by side. When you move, just break down the individual pieces and take them with you. It's this flexibility that makes modular systems so popular.

What makes all this possible? Uprights and components are all designed to fit a so-called "32-millimeter" grid. In other words, uprights, typically spaced about 24 or 32 inches apart, are drilled with double rows of holes every 32 millimeters (see facing page); shelf supports, drawer guides, door hinges, and even cabinet boxes plug right into these holes.

A LOOK AT CLASSIC COMPONENTS

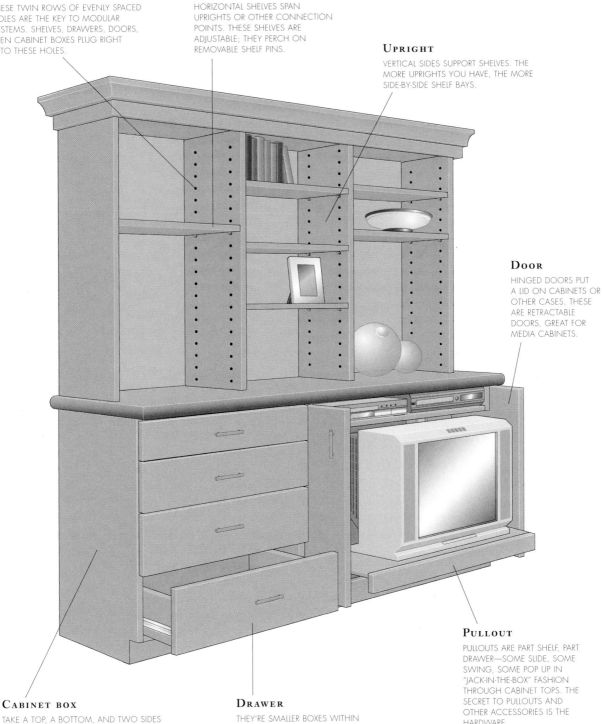

32-MILLIMETER GRID

THESE TWIN ROWS OF EVENLY SPACED HOLES ARE THE KEY TO MODULAR SYSTEMS. SHELVES, DRAWERS, DOORS, EVEN CABINET BOXES PLUG RIGHT INTO THESE HOLES.

SHELF

HORIZONTAL SHELVES SPAN UPRIGHTS OR OTHER CONNECTION POINTS. THESE SHELVES ARE ADJUSTABLE; THEY PERCH ON REMOVABLE SHELF PINS.

UPRIGHT

VERTICAL SIDES SUPPORT SHELVES. THE MORE UPRIGHTS YOU HAVE, THE MORE SIDE-BY-SIDE SHELF BAYS.

DOOR

HINGED DOORS PUT A LID ON CABINETS OR OTHER CASES. THESE ARE RETRACTABLE DOORS, GREAT FOR MEDIA CABINETS.

CABINET BOX

TAKE A TOP, A BOTTOM, AND TWO SIDES AND ADD A BACK—NOW YOU HAVE A CABINET BOX OR "CARCASE."

DRAWER

THEY'RE SMALLER BOXES WITHIN CABINET BOXES, AND THEY SLIDE IN AND OUT ON SLEEK METAL GUIDES OR OTHER RUNNERS.

PULLOUT

PULLOUTS ARE PART SHELF, PART DRAWER—SOME SLIDE, SOME SWING, SOME POP UP IN "JACK-IN-THE-BOX" FASHION THROUGH CABINET TOPS. THE SECRET TO PULLOUTS AND OTHER ACCESSORIES IS THE HARDWARE.

exploring your options

WALL SYSTEMS *come in an almost endless number of versions. You can buy budget pine shelving, fine hardwood cabinetry, a modern laminate library wall, a reproduction Shaker unit, high-end lacquered cabinetry, and scores of other styles. Your options span a wide range of sizes, shapes, and prices.*

Furniture or built-ins?

Broadly speaking, there are two different types of wall systems: furniture pieces and built-ins. To thicken the plot, furniture can be subdivided into traditional freestanding storage pieces and modern modular units. Here's a closer look at the pros and cons of each.

STORAGE FURNITURE. An obvious advantage of freestanding furniture is that it's movable. If it doesn't work in one location or is no longer needed there, you can move it somewhere else. And it goes along with you when you move. Moreover, you can see exactly what you're getting in the store and can usually, though not always, get quick delivery.

One drawback to buying ready-made storage pieces is that you may not always be able to get exactly the size and configuration you want.

MODULAR WALL SYSTEMS. As the name implies, modular components are designed to be mixed and matched—choose the look first, then the shelves, drawers, doors, and other accessories you need. Some modular systems are available "ready-to-assemble" or RTA, and can be broken down flat, moved, then reassembled elsewhere. You can rearrange them or buy additional components as your needs change.

Though buying modular components offers a great deal of flexibility, no system can meet every possible need. Modular systems complement modern room designs well, but if you're looking for a traditional or "unfitted" look, storage pieces or built-ins may be better options.

BUILT-INS. Perhaps the most favored feature of built-ins is that they can look almost seamless in a room. They also allow you to tailor the space precisely to your needs. Though some premade cabinetry can be fitted to look built-in, for the most part, built-ins are customized to your specifications by a cabinetmaker, finish carpenter, or other professional.

Built-ins are particularly well suited to odd-size spaces in your home where a piece of storage furniture can't fit—for example, within a thick wall, under a staircase, over a doorway, and around windows. When they're built into existing walls, they save valuable floor space.

An obvious drawback to built-ins is their expense. Like anything that is custom-made, a built-in unit can be very costly, though the price will vary depending on size, materials, and the complexity of the design. However, built-ins are considered permanent improvements that can return value when you sell your home.

F R E E S T A N D I N G

M O D U L A R

What's your style?

Because of their sheer size, wall systems generally play a major role in a room's design. Do you want a mixed, open look, with shelves, display cubbies, and staggered lines? A quirky, one-of-a-kind painted piece? Or a monolithic wall where storage vanishes behind seamless, lacquered doors and drawer fronts?

Whether you buy premade furniture or build a custom unit, you can create a look that matches any decor. American country pieces, for example, typically have simple lines with sparse, unpretentious detailing. Contemporary pieces, while also characterized by simple, clean lines, are strong and sophisticated, with form often taking precedence over decoration. On the other hand, ornate moldings and carved door and drawer fronts lend old-world charm.

Color can be used to express style, too. For a sleek, sophisticated appearance, choose black, in either a matte or shiny finish. Wood tones, from light to dark, are characteristic of a more traditional style, but a unit painted white will also enhance a traditional living room. For a fresh, contemporary look, consider a bright color.

B U I L T - I N

Material matters

Most wall systems are made of a veneer of wood or laminate over a core of particleboard, medium-density fiberboard, or plywood. A few systems are made of solid wood. Glass is popular for formal display shelves, and some utility units are made from metals or molded plastics. For a closer look at materials not made from wood, see "A Shopper's Guide," beginning on page 87.

SHEET PRODUCTS. Wide panels are generally much more affordable than solid lumber because they require less handwork and utilize wood by-products for the panel cores. Options include particleboard, medium-density fiberboard, and hardwood-veneered plywood.

Workaday, unfinished particleboard is at the low end of the totem pole; choose it for utility cabinets or shelves. Particleboard is made from chips of waste wood—in fact, it's often called "chipboard." It has a roughly speckled appearance, as shown below. Particleboard tends to warp around moisture and can sag under its own weight, so keep shelf spans short (see page 16). Medium-density fiberboard (MDF)—a stronger, smoother cousin to particleboard—stays flatter, can be shaped, and takes paint very well. Both particleboard and MDF are commonly used as substrates for laminates (see below). They're both quite heavy.

Plywood is the most "woodlike" and, in most cases, the priciest sheet product. Plywood is built up from an odd number of thin layers, each peeled from a log and placed perpendicular to the layers above and below. This makes plywood panels more stable than solid lumber and also less likely to warp. Plywood used for wall systems and shelving is usually surfaced on front and back with attractive hardwood veneers, such as oak, maple, ash, or cherry. It comes in various qualities or grades, depending on appearance. The front edges of plywood panels need edge-banding or other trim to mask the raw inner layers.

MELAMINE

MEDIUM-DENSITY
FIBERBOARD (MDF)

PARTICLEBOARD

LAMINATES. Because they're durable, easy to clean, and available in a wide range of colors and patterns, plastic laminates and films are popular surfacing materials for wall systems.

The laminate that covers the core (either particleboard or, for premium products, MDF) is applied in one of three ways. The cheapest and least durable method utilizes a vinyl or paper surface film. This film, available in a range of colors and simulated wood grains, is very thin and can peel away from the core panel.

The next grade of product is melamine, a layer of special paper impregnated with melamine resin. Because it's relatively durable and affordable, this material is quite common. It, too, is sold in many colors and patterns.

Thicker high-pressure laminates are the most durable and costly of the group. These materials come in many colors, patterns, textures, and finishes. Some are appropriate for flat (countertop) surfaces; others are specified only for vertical planes, such as cabinet doors or sides.

SOLID LUMBER. Wood gives a warm, natural look that's hard to match with veneers. Solid wood is more durable, more elegant, and, not surprisingly, much more expensive than most laminates or wood veneer.

Hardwoods (deciduous trees) generally make more precise joints, hold fasteners better, and are more resistant to wear than softwoods (conifers). Hardwood species favored for furniture include light-toned woods, like oak, ash, maple, beech, and birch, and dark-toned species, like cherry, walnut, and mahogany. Alder, poplar, and aspen are budget-minded hardwoods, good for a stained or painted finish.

Most softwoods are less expensive, easier to tool, and more readily available than hardwoods. Pine and fir are the most common. Vertical-grained fir is a beautiful, relatively hard softwood that's normally clear-finished. Knotty pines are often chosen specifically for pickling or waxing when a casual or country look is desired. Otherwise, softwoods normally are painted.

MAPLE PLYWOOD

KNOTTY PINE

OAK

CHERRY

WALNUT

a planning primer

a little engineering

EVEN THE MOST *elaborate wall system won't work if it doesn't provide the right spaces in the right places for the items you need to corral. Plan to keep frequently used items readily accessible: on easily reached shelves, in shallow drawers, or at the front of cabinets. Seldom-used objects can be kept on very low or very high shelves or toward the back of cabinets.*

Remember to take into account objects' sizes and shapes and whether your needs are likely to change in the future. Particularly heavy objects demand strong shelves; for information, see page 16.

SOME IDEAL DIMENSIONS

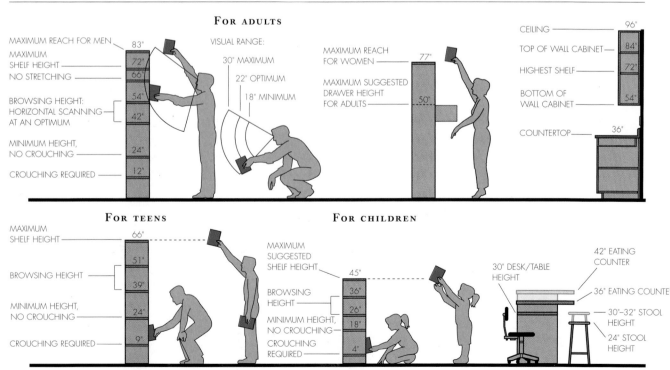

Design guidelines

The drawings on the facing page show norms for fitting wall systems to people. While they're not strict rules, they're good starting points when designing your system.

Don't place shelves out of reach—note that the recommended height for the highest shelf is 6 feet, unless you have a ladder or stool to help you reach its contents. On a similar theme, it's tough for the average adult to see inside a drawer that's over 50 inches off the ground. Also, be aware that accessing extra-low shelves and drawers can require uncomfortable crouching.

Usually, books are stored on open shelving where they can be easily seen and reached. In general, it's best to place heavy books and reference works on the lower tiers of a shelf system. Art books can go at eye level, and paperbacks can be arranged on higher shelves.

Bookshelf space should be a minimum of 9 inches high and 8 inches deep for books of average size. Larger volumes may require shelf space 12 inches high and deep. TV and A/V units usually need 16 to 24 inches of depth.

Though square footage is a good measure of floor space, think in terms of linear footage when figuring your shelving needs. A single shelf 6 feet long offers 6 linear feet of storage. A tall unit with six shelves, each 6 feet long, offers 36 linear feet of storage.

To get a rough idea of the linear footage of shelving you need, simply measure the linear footage of the books, collectibles, and other items you intend to store. If you're building bookshelves, figure 8 to 10 books per running foot of shelving. Allow extra room for expansion and open display space.

Shelf depth and height depend on the size of the objects you intend to put there. Adjustable shelves offer the most flexibility. To determine the right height for fixed shelves, measure the objects that will go there and add an inch or two for head space. The drawings below show the amount of space some common items require.

TYPICAL SIZES OF BOOKS, DISCS, RECORDS, AND TAPES

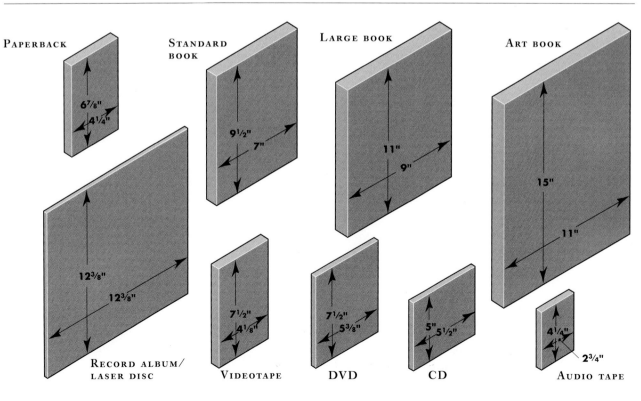

PAPERBACK — $6^{7}/_{8}"$ × $4^{1}/_{4}"$

STANDARD BOOK — $9^{1}/_{2}"$ × $7"$

LARGE BOOK — $11"$ × $9"$

ART BOOK — $15"$ × $11"$

RECORD ALBUM/LASER DISC — $12^{3}/_{8}"$ × $12^{3}/_{8}"$

VIDEOTAPE — $7^{1}/_{2}"$ × $4^{1}/_{8}"$

DVD — $7^{1}/_{2}"$ × $5^{3}/_{8}"$

CD — $5"$ × $5^{1}/_{2}"$

AUDIO TAPE — $4^{1}/_{4}"$ × $2^{3}/_{4}"$

Shelf loads

You don't need to be a structural engineer to design and assemble your own shelves. Still, some fundamental principles should be observed.

The drawing below shows four basic ways to make a shelf; the one you should choose will depend on the expected load. To avoid a sagging shelf, always be conservative; use the stoutest construction you can.

For light loads (paperback books, small art objects, stemware), 1-by pine or fir (¾-inch thick) or ¾-inch sheet products up to 32 inches long work fine. For medium loads (art books, vases, some audio gear), you're better off going to thicker lumber. If you want to stick to ¾-inch stock, shorten the shelf to 24 or even 16 inches; you can also reinforce the shelf edges, as shown.

Be especially cautious with heavy loads (wine racks, TVs, large audio rigs). Use 2-by lumber, two layers of plywood, or, even better, a solid-lumber web frame with plywood top and bottom.

MAXIMUM SPANS BETWEEN SUPPORTS

Note: Reduce all spans for heavy loads. Glass shelves are sized for lightweight loads only.

Material	Span (inches)
1-by (¾-inch) pine or fir	32
2-by (1½-inch) pine or fir	48
1-inch hardwood	48
¾-inch plywood-core veneer or laminate	32
¾-inch particleboard-core veneer or laminate	24
¼-inch plate glass (12 inches deep)	36
⅜-inch plate glass (12 inches deep)	48
½-inch plate glass (12 inches deep)	60

FOUR WAYS TO MAKE A SHELF

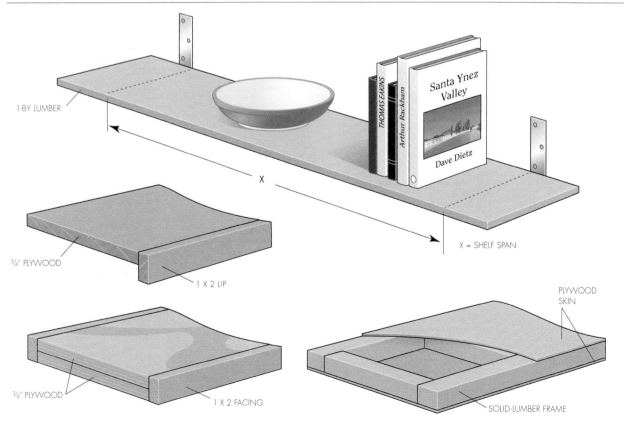

1-BY LUMBER

X

X = SHELF SPAN

¾" PLYWOOD

1 X 2 LIP

¾" PLYWOOD

1 X 2 FACING

PLYWOOD SKIN

SOLID-LUMBER FRAME

Make connections

Regardless of their appearance, remember that all wall systems consist at least of horizontals supported by verticals. Shelves can be supported from the floor, wall, or ceiling, but the basic geometry remains the same.

The simplest open shelves may require only wood or metal wall brackets, L-braces, or other "floating" hardware. For details, see pages 90–91.

Formal uprights can be made from ¾-inch sheet materials or 1-by or 2-by solid lumber. The load-carrying capacity depends more on the shelf-to-upright connection than on the thickness of the uprights.

Shelves may be fixed or adjustable, depending on your attachment method. Shown at right are four common fixed-shelf connections. Simple butt joints, glued and nailed or screwed, will suffice for light duty; biscuits or cleats add strength. Dadoed construction provides strong joints and adds rigidity to backless shelving units.

There are many different types of adjustable shelf connectors; the most popular are shown at right. Tracks and brackets are for open walls; tracks and clips, shelf pins, and other items connect shelves to uprights.

NEED HELP?

If you're uncertain about designing, building, and/or installing a wall system yourself, you may want to enlist the help of others who are experts at their trades. Here's a list of some professionals who can help:

- Architects
- Interior designers and decorators
- Furniture and wall system retailers
- Custom cabinetmakers
- Finish carpenters
- Media specialists

BASIC SHELF CONNECTIONS

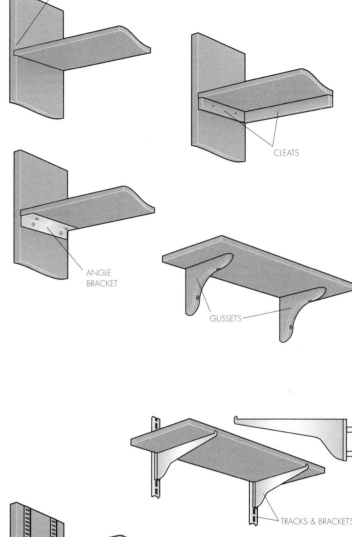

DADO JOINT

CLEATS

ANGLE BRACKET

GUSSETS

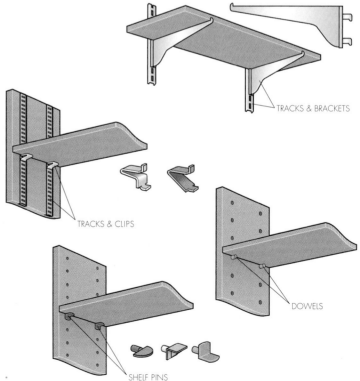

TRACKS & BRACKETS

TRACKS & CLIPS

DOWELS

SHELF PINS

a home for electronics

WITH THE *surging tide of surround-sound, high-definition televisions, DVDs, and other digital innovations in our lives, organizing and storing audiovisual gear has become a high priority in many of today's homes. It's also one of the most popular uses for wall systems.*

Because the design of a large media center is critical to its function, you may want help. Be sure the designer you select has experience working with electronics or will consult with A/V experts.

Some basic checkpoints

"Home theater" might mean a DVD player and a large-screen television, or it could mean the real deal—projection screen, audiovisual receiver, and six or more speakers. Obviously, your storage strategy depends on which of these approaches you're leaning toward.

When it comes to organizing basic electronic equipment and accessories, nearly any type of unit will work, from a ready-made media cabinet to storage furniture, and from a modular system to custom cabinetry. For the most flexibility, look for a unit with adjustable shelving.

Shelving units with open backs provide the ventilation demanded by many electronic components. With adequate ventilation, cabinets work just as well as open shelving. They also help hide stacks of tapes, compact discs, vintage vinyl, and other paraphernalia, and keep them dust-free.

You'll need to decide whether to showcase your gear or hide it. Perhaps you want to recess the entire unit into the wall and cover it with speaker cloth. You can now buy infrared receiver units that allow you to use remote controls with cabinet doors closed.

Another consideration: flashy lines and colors can distract from the home-theater experience. When the lights go down, the unit should be merely background.

Whether you're buying ready-made furniture or designing your own built-in, remember that a television or other similar equipment can be very heavy. Be sure shelf and platform materials can support the weight (for information, see pages 16–17).

Choosing a location

Finding the right spot for your equipment isn't always easy. Though the family room may seem an obvious choice, especially for a television, audio components can go almost anywhere, as long as you can run wires from the equipment to speakers located in other parts of the house.

Often televisions are placed as afterthoughts when, in reality, they may be the room's main

feature. If space is limited, a corner wall unit for video and audio equipment can visually anchor it, gearing the area for both entertainment and conversation.

The shape, size, lighting, and acoustics of a room will all affect its performance. For a true home-theater environment, the room should be at least 10 by 14 feet. Also, take into account any glare from windows that could affect viewing. Subdued, neutral room colors are best for a home-theater environment.

Make sure there's sufficient lighting in the area to see titles on CDs and tapes and read equipment controls. If you're building a custom unit, consider including an interior lighting system. Because fluorescent light may cause interference, plan other light sources near a tuner or receiver. Some low-voltage dimmers and transformers may also cause buzzing. For more information on lighting, see page 124.

The epitome of a built-in wall system, this home theater setup boasts screen, projector, and surround-sound speakers (above). Moviegoers here are cushioned in comfort— with their feet up. The projector is suspended unobtrusively from the ceiling, and audiovisual gear is concealed in a nearby closet (left).

A HOME THEATER OVERVIEW

What transforms a TV, a VCR, and a bunch of other black boxes into a formal home theater? It's the systematic relationship between several key devices, all tied together with low-voltage wires and cables.

Typical home theater components are shown below. The television and speakers are the obvious stars, but it's the audiovisual receiver that's really "command central." A plethora of media signals may be routed to the A/V receiver from components both inside and outside the home: a cable box, satellite dish, off-the-air antenna, VCR, or DVD player. The receiver allows you to choose which of these input sources you want, and then encodes and outputs signals to the TV and speakers. Consider the A/V receiver as the axis of whatever scheme you're planning.

■ **Video options.** Television monitors are available in a growing number of versions: direct view, rear projection, front projection, flat screen or plasma, and high definition. You'll need some showroom help unraveling your options; and, just as important, you'll need cable and wiring connections that are compatible with your A/V receiver.

■ **Audio aspects.** Surround sound is the heart of the home theater experience. A battery of at least five and often six speakers is driven by digital encoding supplied by the A/V receiver. Matching speakers at front left and front right provide "stereo." A shielded center speaker, mounted above the TV or placed right on top, fills in the middle. (You could use the TV's built-in speaker, but a separate center speaker usually sounds better.) Left-rear and right-rear speakers create the surround-sound effect. In addition, a sixth speaker—a specialized subwoofer—is often placed at rear center (although technically it could be placed anywhere, as these low-frequency sounds have no clear "direction").

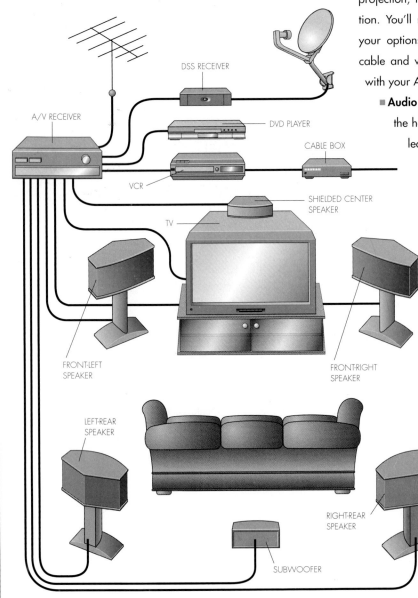

DSS RECEIVER

A/V RECEIVER

DVD PLAYER

CABLE BOX

VCR

SHIELDED CENTER SPEAKER

TV

FRONT-LEFT SPEAKER

FRONT-RIGHT SPEAKER

LEFT-REAR SPEAKER

RIGHT-REAR SPEAKER

SUBWOOFER

Equipment checklist

To plan your A/V setup, begin by making a list of the components you own and those you may want to add later, and note their measurements. Also count up your accoutrements, such as compact discs, vintage vinyl, and accessories. Decide what you'll house in the wall system and what components (speakers, for example) need to be nearby.

TELEVISIONS. Today's television sets can be tough to plan for—they're big, heavy, and most stick way out in back. The simplest large-screen storage solution is a low TV stand (shown below); some models roll on wheels, while others pivot.

Cabinet-housed TVs require sturdy shelves and extra depth. For a television that's not too heavy, consider a special TV shelf that pulls out of the cabinet and swivels for convenient viewing. A pullout shelf can also accommodate a lazy Susan or turntable (for details, see page 108). You can also buy TV lifts that pop up through a base cabinet.

Make sure that the doors on a television cabinet swing open far enough so they don't obstruct your view, or use retractable doors.

COMPONENTS. Do you like the open-rack look or closed cabinets? You'll want components placed conveniently and accessibly, protected from overheating, and situated for optimal performance.

Pay strict attention to the manufacturer's recommendations, particularly in regard to ventilation. Though ventilation grilles (see page 110) at the back and top of a unit might suffice, you may need to install an exhaust fan if several

CD ORGANIZER

CD TABLE RACKS

pieces of equipment are grouped in one tight enclosure.

TAPES, RECORDS, AND COMPACT DISCS. For small items such as compact discs and cassette tapes, divided drawers offer the most efficient storage. You can get a lot of CDs in one drawer! For easy access, don't place drawers much higher than waist level. If you don't have room for drawers, commercial organizers can keep your tapes, compact discs, records, and accessories in order. Place tapes, compact discs, DVDs, laser discs, and vinyl away from direct sunlight and other heat sources.

SPEAKERS. Unless your speakers are the so-called "shielded" type, be sure they're located at least 12 inches from the television screen to prevent picture distortion. For optimum stereo separation, speakers need to be at least 5 feet away from each other.

Recessed wall speakers look neat and reduce clutter; other options include wall mounts, bookshelf mounts, and cabinet-housed speakers and components hidden behind larger sweeps of speaker cloth.

COMPONENT CABINET

TV STAND

room-by-room solutions

WHEN IT COMES *to wall systems, every room in the house is fair game. Look carefully at each room's layout and the areas suitable for display and storage. Also browse through the scores of storage solutions in the next chapter, "Great Wall Systems," beginning on page 27. Ready to go? Here are some room-by-room guidelines to get you started.*

Living spaces

Whether you and your family congregate in an informal living room, a family room, a great room, or a den, that's the place where activities such as reading, watching television, game playing, and listening to music occur. Every one of those activities invites clutter.

The best living-room units are often a mixture of closed storage and open display niches. Lighting is important here—accent light for pictures and collectibles and ambient light to access storage items. A two-sided room divider can double your storage frontage and redefine a sprawling floor plan.

Because they're so versatile, modular wall systems are popular in living areas. Equipped with adjustable shelving, cabinets, drawers, television bays, and other specialty options, these units can organize myriad objects.

But virtually any piece of storage furniture can help contain the clutter.

How about a hand-painted pine bookcase? An antique armoire? Or, a deep central media unit with flanking side towers?

In more formal living areas, built-ins offer display and storage opportunities. A built-in that combines open shelving and cabinets can exhibit art objects and prized collectibles as well as conceal audio equipment and accessories.

Dining rooms

An armoire, hutch, or other freestanding cupboard or cabinet with glass or solid doors provides plenty of space for china and glassware and also helps keep them dust-free. Built-in units that include drawers, adjustable shelves, and cabinets are also good organizers. Stacks of dishes can be very heavy, so be sure shelves are strong and well-supported. When a low-profile unit is combined with a countertop, it also provides a buffet-style serving area.

If the dining area is part of a large kitchen or an extension of your living room, a wall system—floor to ceiling or just waist high—can effectively divide the space and create the effect of a separate dining room.

Where space is at a premium, a dining room that's used only part-time for meals can serve

LIVING-ROOM MEDIA CENTER

DINING-ROOM DIVIDER

other roles as well. A wall system outfitted with a fold-down desk, file drawers, and cabinets can provide efficient office space that's camouflaged when company arrives. Or how about a cabinet filled with audio equipment wired to speakers throughout the house?

Kitchens

Today, it's acknowledged that the kitchen is the hub of most homes, especially those with open or "great-room" floor plans. So it stands to reason that the concepts of kitchen storage and display are being stretched, too. Computers, video games, collections, and sewing centers are all part of the picture.

Display niches warm an otherwise blank stretch of cabinets. What about glass-fronted

KITCHEN DISPLAY SOFFIT

wall cabinets lit by built-in, low-voltage light fixtures? If you're worried about keeping things tidy, opt for translucent instead of clear glass. Or add a stand-alone display cabinet or recycled hutch. Don't overlook over-cabinet soffits, and consider glass shelves against a window. Flipper doors, fold-down doors, pullout shelves, and roll-around shelf units keep items tucked away when not in use.

Kitchen transition zones—spots between the main work triangle and other living spaces—are prime terrain for cubbyholes or a computer desk, an A/V rack, or a swiveling TV pullout.

Bedrooms and closets

Today's bedrooms are more than just rooms of repose. Master suites may include audio and video gear, fitness equipment, home office alcoves, reading nooks, sitting areas with fire-places, and more.

Where space is limited in bedrooms, wall systems that store both clothing and other gear are particu-larly useful. For example, a large wall unit can stand in for conventional dress-ers. What about a built-in headboard with wrap-around shelving? Or a freestanding room divider with headboard on one side and dresser drawers on the other?

Guest bedrooms often double as offices or media rooms. A seamless, com-mercial wall system is a natural here, with built-in pullouts, fold-down work-table, and, perhaps, a Murphy bed.

BEDROOM BUILT-IN

Closets—especially those designated areas in master suites—can benefit from a wall system's organizing touch, too.

Bathrooms

Like bedrooms, bathrooms are dancing new steps, becoming bigger, multiuse retreats. Even small, traditional baths can benefit from fresh takes on storage and display.

Pedestal sinks are hot, but cost you the vanity storage below standard deck-mounted fixtures. So look to the walls: a mix of open and closed storage makes a bathroom seem less closed in and more energetic. Recessed storage is a good choice. Or stack up a storage tower with closed drawers, open shelves or ladders for colorful towels, and maybe some pantry pullouts.

When choosing commercial units, watch out for cheap laminates; they're easy to clean but susceptible to moisture damage. If you're using glass in the bath, make sure it's tempered safety glass. Whatever bathroom unit you opt for, good room ventilation is a must.

KIDS' ROOM CORRAL

Kids' rooms

In children's rooms, flexibility is the key. Look for modular systems and accessories that can be raised or reconfigured as children grow. Units that bundle low bookshelves, a desk, and drawers together save space and encourage neatness. Some systems include the bed, too.

Bins, baskets, pegs, hooks, and stackable storage cubes are naturals for casual spaces. If you opt for open shelves, make them adjustable. Rolling carts and other mobile bins and shelving allow kids—and their parents—to custom-tailor space as projects and play require.

Home offices

Do you want closed storage or open display? It partially depends on whether you have a stand-alone space or are trying to tuck an office into another room. Often, a mix of open and closed storage is best. Remember that it's your home, not just an office, and choose styles and materials accordingly. Display niches and art pieces help personalize your workspace.

Commercial wall systems can create a seamless, efficient office area, fusing desk, credenza, shelves, computer and printer

BATHROOM DISPLAY NICHE

pullouts, and copious file drawers into one unit. Or select stand-alones like the classic rolltop desk, converted office armoire, and roll-around file cart. If you have the space and budget, built-in library cases can supply a traditional "study" style.

Hallways and stairs

Here it's all about found space; for colorful ideas, see pages 76–81. Stairways are prime targets: under-stair shelves, pullouts, and tansu drawers are classics. Look also to stair landings, where a little extra depth can make way for a built-in library. Recessed display niches add spark along the stairs' path.

Recessed built-ins are also good solutions for some hallways. To find space to add bookshelves or display niches, look up high or consider an end wall.

Think lighting when you're considering these found spaces. Most hallways and stairs are not as brightly lit as other living spaces, so you'll probably need to add some accent or task fixtures (see page 124).

HOME OFFICE BOOK WALL

Utility areas

Laundry rooms, workrooms, garages, and other functional zones of the home can use shelving and cabinetry to keep tools and supplies organized. Because access is often more important than aesthetics in these areas, utility shelves and cabinets are usually sufficient for general storage.

Most home centers stock lines of modular utility units made from melamine or raw particleboard. Typical components include shelves, base cabinets, tall tool cabinets, drawers, worktables, and open shelves. Add a wall organizer, hooks, or an industrial shelving unit, and you're in business. Budget-priced wall cabinets from the kitchen department work here, too.

Vinyl-coated wire shelves, bins, and baskets are naturals for laundry rooms. For details, see pages 114–115.

UNDER-STAIR CUBBIES

LAUNDRY SHELVES AND BINS

GREAT WALL SYSTEMS

NEED INSPIRATION? This chapter is packed with colorful examples of different wall systems, from basic movable shelves and shelf units to traditional furniture pieces and up-to-the-minute media centers. We've included great ideas for just about every storage and display need. All are designed to set you thinking about how to solve your own storage and styling challenges. **AS YOU PERUSE THESE PAGES,** study what materials were used and how the design relates to the room. Note also where the units are placed and how particular objects are displayed or stored in them. Though many of the wall systems shown were designed for a particular area and purpose, don't let that stop you—you can adapt them to nearly any situation. **FOR SPECIFIC** room-by-room guidelines, turn back to pages 22–25. See some hardware, component, or shelf lumber that piques your interest? Check out "A Shopper's Guide," beginning on page 87, for details.

great wall systems

simply shelves

OPEN SHELVES are handy and easy to install, and most have a certain wide-eyed charm. They don't dominate a room the way more complex wall units can.

Choose your shelves from solid wood, sheet products, glass, or metal in stock, custom, or homemade designs. For starters, you'll need to make sure the shelves and shelving hardware are strong enough for the weight you're piling on them. For guidelines, see pages 14–17. Besides providing extra strength, thicker shelves have a bolder profile that complements some styles.

Shelf connections are adjustable or fixed. Some hardware is standard in home centers: tracks and brackets, tracks and clips, and at least a few types of shelf pins that fit in drilled holes. Fixed hardware includes cleats, gussets, and angle brackets. Torsion boxes and other "floating" shelves are fixed and have no visible hardware. For a closer look at all these items, see pages 88–93.

A shelf unit requires side supports and maybe a back. Some designs are anchored to the wall; others aren't. The shelves may or may not be adjustable. Many systems are modular. You can even put a unit on wheels and roll it to the task.

Before you resolve to fill all your storage needs with shelves, be sure you want all that open storage. You'll be looking at those items all the time, even when they're dusty or disorganized. Sometimes, it's best to mix it up, choosing open shelves for display and things you use a lot, and drawers and cabinets for items you'd rather hide.

Why not roll the shelves to the task? This movable cart features industrial-strength steel shelves— plus a quartet of heavy-duty casters.

Dark-stained wood shelves float beside a kitchen pass-through, supporting both colorful, glazed 1950s pottery and working goods. The floating boxes are supported from behind by invisible, cantilevered hardware.

*Simple and traditional, the kitchen scheme above
features curved wood gussets and wall cleats that
prop up 1-by shelves lipped with stronger 1 by 2s.
All components are painted a clean, classic white.*

*Some shelves do double duty: this one organizes
children's clothes and offers a secure perch for
a household frog. The traditional design—
called a peg rail—is comprised of wall ledger,
inset wooden pegs (you could also use metal
hooks), top shelf, and side gussets.*

Clear, curved shelving displays a collection of art glass in bright hues from around the color ring. Barely noticeable supporting hardware hangs from a metal-laminate soffit.

Simple flat shelves bridge commercial track-and-bracket hardware. You can buy the pieces at a home center. Anchor vertical tracks to wall framing, insert brackets, lay a commercial shelf—or one of your own—across them, and you're done.

Maybe you don't even need a shelf. These floating perches, with formal crown molding profiles, are just deep enough for pictures and paintings—much like a classic picture rail.

Magazines are always hard to keep a handle on, but the open rack shown at right can help. This home office space also sports a bookcase on wheels; just give a tug and pull it where you want.

Serious cooking requires serious shelving, and this all-steel gourmet unit is ready for the work-load. Part display and part industrial, many of these strong, stylish units offer modular components that can be mixed and matched to fit your needs.

Anything you can stably stack becomes a shelving unit. At left, a set of matching wooden benches was covered with multiple paint layers, then sanded and abraded for an antique, distressed look.

Freestanding shelf ladders made of soldered copper pipe and fittings create a vivid, contemporary display wall with a whimsical space for the television set right in the middle.

Curving glass shelves lend a bright, open feel to this combination pass-through/display niche. The clear glass allows the halogen accent light to shine down unhindered from shelf to shelf.

A fir bookcase sits on a bright blue wall above the piano. The wall unit, with trim strips on front of shelves and vertical pilasters to match, has no visible hanging hardware to mar the clean lines.

Serenity comes to the master bath in the form of these clean, simple display shelves, which are wall-mounted to float like the bench. Honey-toned hemlock adds a warm glow.

hardworking walls

THE JUMP from open shelves to wall systems is one of both style and function. Although wall systems may simply formalize shelves, such as in the case of a large wall of books, they may also incorporate cabinet frames, doors, drawers, pullouts, and other add-on accessories. These latter components vary the look of shelves and make them more useful.

What if you own stacks and stacks of books? It's no problem to go higher if you have the headroom— plus a solid library ladder to scale those heights.

Some wall systems shown here are freestanding pieces, while others are built-ins (for more on built-ins, see pages 48–53). Book walls can be positioned as high as you like, but remember that you'll need access to the upper levels; note the library ladders shown on these two pages. Modular systems abound, as do your choices in furniture components, kitchen cabinets, and media units. All of these options are addressed in the chapter "A Shopper's Guide," beginning on page 87.

Add doors to a set of bookshelves and you have a wall system of cabinets. The key architectural feature of this family room is an enlarged, built-in, stepped tansu surrounding the fireplace. The sandalwood-finished maple cabinets house the entertainment system and provide tidy storage for discs, tapes, and books.

To reach a happy ending, it's usually best to think of a large wall system as an integral part of your room's design, not just an add-on. Strive to keep the look uncluttered, but also vary components to break the monotony of a potentially blank wall. Display niches (see pages 54–59), staggered lines, and choices of both materials and finishes make huge differences in the visual weight of your hardworking wall.

White, formal surroundings call for a built-in book
wall to match. In this case, the entire wall is built out
into the room, and the shelf bays are recessed in the
resulting space. Wide, flat trim frames the space, echoing
the arched entry door and the built-up ceiling bays.

Boxlike cherry wall cabinets, some open for display,
establish this family room's rectilinear frame. With a
vivid palette of purple, raspberry, emerald, and teal
sprinkled throughout, the cabinets offer plenty of room
for storage, display, and a computer desk.

This combination sitting room, media space, and display gallery is all tied together with wall systems. The open knee-wall shelf curves to follow the window bay, leading the eye toward the fireplace-flanking open shelves and closed, Euro-style cabinets.

Handsome, vertical veneers wrap around seamless home office built-ins, integrating bookshelves, display spaces, and an extra-tall soffit area above window level. Note the floating kickspace below the units, which are anchored to the wall, not the floor.

Part room, part wall system, this walk-in window seat alcove has built-ins throughout. Shelves flank the doorway and ring the window, and drawers pull out below the cushion. Black backs on shelf bays add depth and contrast to display items.

As the focal point of an open, comfortable master suite, this striking cedar storage wall divides bedroom from bath and also functions as a headboard.

A unit of walnut cubes forms this built-in headboard. Cubes are solid in the actual headboard section, form square display cubbies elsewhere, and blend right in with the adjacent doors and door trim. The unit is wired with phone jacks and electrical outlets.

Furniture-grade cherry forms a hardworking but great-looking storage wall in a transition zone between kitchen and living room. Cabinets combine open shelves, soffit niches, and closed pantry doors below with textured glass above—a striking mix of open, closed, and partially veiled storage and display space.

Hardworking walls are a big plus in the bathroom, where space is always lacking. This storage wall combines plenty of drawer space with amenities like glass display shelves, arched soffit trim, fluted vertical pilasters, and the traditional touch of beaded boards in the open case back.

great wall systems

unfitted furnishings

THE SEAMLESS LOOK is one option; the other time-honored approach is to use individual, freestanding pieces. This unfitted style is especially apt in casual, eclectic, or period settings—or anywhere a looser look or floor plan is desired. It also makes it much easier to mix and match storage pieces you might find along the way.

Furniture stores stock many freestanding designs. For shopping tips, see pages 100–103. Home-improvement warehouses, retail shops, and mail-order catalogs offer an increasing number of storage and display units.

There are other possibilities, too. What about an antique hutch, armoire, or credenza? Or a stack of recycled straw baskets, wire bins, or storage cubes? Scour thrift stores and garage sales for storage subjects in a broad range of colors and textures. Or look for pieces to decorate yourself.

Unfinished freestanding pieces—typically built from pine or budget hardwoods like alder or poplar—offer an almost blank canvas for personal expression. Stain a bookcase, paint it white, or paint each shelf a different hue. Pickle that armoire, apply a crackle finish, or "age" and distress the doors with sandpaper, file, or even a hammer. You could also strip and refinish an old flea-market find—who knows what lies underneath?

It's your basic free-standing bookcase, but with some personalized touches: floating vertical dividers, a swirling decorative finish, and a swimming fish medallion at the top.

An antique pine hutch makes the perfect backdrop for an antique dining table. The hutch shows off a fine collection of majolica—distinctly glazed earthenware featuring shapes and motifs from nature.

Freestanding boxes and cubes—
including colorful doors, drawer
fronts, and open, see-through shelf
bays—can be stacked and rotated
atop one another. Flat, matching
countertops float atop the unit.
This assemblage doubles as a
kids' room divider and personal
"fortress."

Bright red barrister cases with
glass-front doors are stacked to form
a lively mix of storage and display.
The individual boxes sit atop an
integral base with decorative legs.

A lot of "found" items can be stacked or recycled as wall systems. At left, a former library card catalog is now labeled for kitchen utensils.

The ornamental, ladderlike shelf unit above houses pullout rattan baskets.

Corners are often prime space wasters, so why not tailor a wall unit to use this area? This trim, triangular dining-room piece was finished with pickled white paint, which was then partially rubbed away for an aged effect.

great wall systems

beautiful built-ins

ON THE FAR SIDE of the fence from freestanding pieces are so-called built-ins. A built-in unit that forms an integral part of the room's architecture can save a lot of space. It can also look like it belongs in the room in a way that more casual pieces may not—especially in formal or modern settings.

As you thumb through the following pages, note how both the materials and the trimmings interact with the room designs. Baseboards that ring a room continue on below built-in units; integral ceiling or crown moldings likewise tie areas together. Some units are clearly made of wood, while others seem to blend with the wall materials: wallboard, plaster, or tile.

While many so-called "built-ins" are actually built into the wall, others are really built out from the wall. Schemes range from simple, between-stud wall recesses to those that entail reframing the entire wall to surround the built-in.

Most built-ins are custom-fitted, but you could take stock units and either recess them or fill in around them with new wall coverings. In either case, moldings surrounding the opening blend the new and old.

Custom units allow great flexibility in terms of both materials and details like doors, drawers, or glass-shelved display "windows." You can also purchase specialty accessories (see pages 118–121) to plug into custom or commercial built-ins. Light fixtures (see page 124) and A/V wires are much simpler to incorporate into built-ins than into some stand-alone pieces.

A shallow recessed niche at one end of the kitchen counter displays earthenware pottery in all of the home's palette colors. The tile-lined alcove sports a single, distressed wood shelf.

A contemporary room design is highlighted by fireside built-ins. Recessed plaster niches on top have spotlights to accent display pieces. Downlights embedded in plaster soffits shine down and through glass shelves, washing collectibles below.

A decorative glass window is framed by warm-toned wood built-ins. Note how heavy-profiled baseboards and crown moldings tie all the components together.

A hardworking storage cube is lined with brightly painted beaded paneling, and accented with decorative wrought-iron hinges and hardware. The box houses adjustable book-shelves, an open phone niche, and ample closed storage to the right.

An amply sized foyer can do double duty as a family library or home office when outfitted with built-ins. These shelves frame an interior passage, creating an extra-thick wall or tunnel.

Square, recessed display niches and other custom
touches, usually reserved for formal living rooms,
dress up this master bedroom's conversation space.
Collectibles are accented by tiny strip lights tucked
behind the top front of each niche.

Burly, fixed timber shelves are the perfect
counterpart to a plastered wall alcove. Note how the
matching baseboards weave in and out of the recessed
space, augmenting the built-in effect.

great wall systems

on display

B OOKSHELVES ARE the perfect vehicle, of course, for storing books. But a wall of solid books can rob a room of interest, visual texture, and decorative focal points. That's why it's often important to break up the monotony with objects worthy of display.

Gather the items you want to display, grouping objects that have something in common, such as color, form, or function. Position adjustable shelves so that they align in an attractive, organized way or form an interesting pattern. You can remove a shelf or two to create spaces for larger objects.

If you need to devote a lot of shelf space to books, avoid placing them wall-to-wall. Instead, shorten the rows, propping books with bookends, and display art objects or other items in the remaining space.

Special pieces may need protection, security, and lighting. A ready-made or built-in unit with glass shelves, sliding glass doors, and interior lighting allows you to enjoy your collection and, at the same time, keep it safe, secure, and clean. Some collectibles can be kept on open shelves; others should be stored in dust-free cabinets or drawers.

Good lighting is critical to many displays. Ceiling-mounted downlights or tracks can highlight any display; built-in options include low-voltage downlights, strip lights, and other discreet fixtures (see page 124).

If you live in an area prone to earthquakes, you might opt for a cabinet with doors that can be locked or latched closed.

Railed, recessed shelving in a colonial-style kitchen holds a collection of blue-patterned chargers and cups from different design traditions.

Bowls and vases seem to hover within this elegant display cabinet. Recessed downlights shine from the top; additional light on a separate switch comes from fiber optics behind the translucent back.

Seamless floor-to-ceiling maple cabinets include velvet-lined display niches. Built-in, low-voltage downlights in each niche highlight collectibles, which seem to leap out of their flat-black backgrounds.

Rich red shelving showcases a collection of majolica plates, pitchers, candlesticks, and pewter accent pieces in a recessed corner cabinet. Glass-paneled doors showcase the contents while keeping them secure and dust-free.

Glass shelves, glass interior doors, and a matching courtyard window in back—this see-through display cabinet is illuminated not only by recessed downlights from above, but also by daylight shining through the windows behind.

great wall systems

Rough, knife-applied plaster dresses up the display niche above and even covers the wood shelves, forming a colorful, casual frame for the collection within.

Discreet metal angle brackets lend support to narrow, scooped shelves, which in turn cradle a collection of classic rolling pins in this gourmet chef's kitchen.

The shelves above float on invisible hardware. Their clean lines are matched by pinpoint lighting, courtesy of low-voltage fixtures with aimable slot apertures.

At left, African art pieces are "framed" behind glass in recessed niches that step down in tandem with the nearby stairs.

media stars

ONE OF THE hottest arenas for wall systems is the media unit or home entertainment center. Besides contemplating cost and looks, you'll need to decide whether you want to feature all those gleaming gizmos or hide them. Do you want freestanding separates, a coordinated modular system, or custom built-ins with handy doors, drawers, and pullouts? Some setups are modest; others, like full-blown home theaters, are dazzlingly complex. Regardless of your specific case, the basic question remains: how do you keep all this stuff from taking over?

First, decide if the system is to be a focal point in your room. The media center often takes the place of the fireplace/hearth as a living-room's focus. If this is your desire, make sure to plan accordingly; if not, then take steps to hide it. You'll see both approaches on these pages.

Popular large-screen televisions can be a major design challenge. How do you house that big rear end or that blank, boring screen? Corner built-ins are one prime option, utilizing an oft-wasted space; pullouts, pop-ups, and turntables can also accommodate a TV's depth. Flipper doors or tambour doors cover the screen when it's not in use. For a closer look at all these items, see pages 108–111.

Remember that it's not just the electronics that need housing, but the CDs, DVDs, cassettes, vintage vinyl, and other media that go along with them. For sizing guidelines, see page 15.

Armoires take up less floor space than some media-center alternatives because they use vertical, rather than horizontal, space. The armoire below conceals a TV.

The sleek, modern lines of this family room center on both the traditional fireplace and the up-to-the-minute home entertainment system. The floor-to-ceiling media unit that joins the black wraparound hearth includes shelf space and display niches, along with a heavy-duty TV and components.

This major, wall-to-wall media system discloses a massive
large-screen television when the sliding doors are open
(top of page). When it's movie time, the doors slide closed and
a projection screen descends (above). A sliding library ladder
helps access the lofty regions of the sturdy wood shelves.

A pair of purple bi-fold doors, hinged vertically with a piano hinge,
open to expose a serious collection of rack-mounted A/V components—
everything from classic turntable to surround-sound receiver.

A wide, plasma-screen TV becomes part of the display, too,

as it floats amidst an open shelf grid.

CD storage can be boring, but not with this unit. The free-form metal "wave" and "bookends" complement the modern color scheme perfectly. You can stack up all the CDs you want—at least until gravity kicks in.

The media center on the facing page could have been overly dominant, but careful detailing helps the design blend in with its surroundings. Made of pine, with hand-pegged doors, the cabinetry features dentil detailing beneath crown molding; the speaker cloth matches the TV screen.

Sometimes television viewing and formal entertaining don't coincide. In this case, however, a corner location not only moved the TV to the side, but also allowed extra cabinet depth to accommodate it. The built-in unit features pocket doors; the TV sits on a swivel mount.

Tucked into a corner below existing beams, this 10- by 14-foot structure sports a simple, serene façade that's covered mostly by sliding shoji screens. A walk-in closet fits behind the entertainment center; its sliding panel allows access to the stereo components.

room dividers

Not all wall systems stand against a wall. Islands and peninsulas that float alone in a room can stretch available wall space, redirect traffic patterns, or even define different areas. Storage-wise, room dividers help you get rid of clutter by consolidating open and closed shelves and cabinets. They also make great media centers.

Room dividers may be short, tall, narrow, or deep. They can be used in any space from great room and dining room to breakfast nook, bedroom, and bath. Short units may be freestanding; taller ones should be firmly anchored to the floor, wall, and/or ceiling. They can be single- or double-sided. For even more storage, pack the protruding end with display niches.

Decide whether your room divider should blend with its surroundings or add some contrasting energy. Should it appear to be built into the room or to be a brash, brightly-stained, furniture piece? Should you tie it in with integral baseboards or crown molding? Consider capping a short base unit with a granite countertop; add a library ladder to a floor-to-ceiling tower.

A bank of blank, closed cabinets can be oppressive, so it's important to mix things up, perhaps by adding see-through windows, glass-paneled doors, display niches, and built-in accent lighting to your storage wall. Or stagger the sizes and shapes of shelves, drawer fronts, and doors.

This cherry-and-marble built-in, housed in a pass-through space, does triple duty as room divider, display shelf, and dining room buffet.

A soaring maple built-in dramatically divides the dining room from the entryway; at the same time, it adds lots of display and storage space. Base cabinets are joined by a glass-doored, glass-shelved wall unit. High soffit lighting shines down on the maple counter below.

A 30-inch-wide
"storage spine"
(below) runs nearly
the length of the house
and acts as a divider
between public and
private spaces.
All storage closets,
cabinets, and drawers
are located here. Turn
the corner (left) and
you'll find a CD
collection on short
shelves. Freeing
perimeter walls of
cabinets gave the
owners much more
room for furniture
and art.

This remodeled storage wall is clean, simple, and colorful—all done on a budget. The cabinets are basic plywood. By painting them in bright colors, the owners made them special. In the living room, they created a built-in display case to showcase art and conceal audio equipment.

A two-sided divider that's part wall, part tower defines an office area and provides a home for office literature and sample products. The ladder slides on its plumbing-pipe top rail, offering access to the unit's upper nooks and crannies.

great wall systems

office ideas

As HOME-OFFICE USE mushrooms, so do new wall-system solutions. Phones, computers, printers, files, bookcases, binder and magazine racks, and big bunches of tangled wires are common parts of the puzzle. But these spaces aren't always just for work; display and even media-center needs are being folded in. Both commercial and custom designs and materials are getting more sophisticated. As they say, it's not just an office; it's your home, too.

Modular systems (pages 104–107) are one popular way to go. You can buy work counters, file cabinets, overhead bins, and platforms for printers, then mix and match them to fit your space. On the other hand, built-ins offer an unmatched opportunity for formal and traditional looks. Either way, you'll find a growing number of high-tech pullouts and computer accessories to choose from; for starters, see pages 118–121. Some office storage is totally open, some totally closed. As usual, a mix of both styles seems to work best, allowing you to camouflage storage chaos while allowing for some custom touches.

Remember that an office can be located anywhere: in a guest room or kitchen alcove, on a stair landing, or inside a former closet. For other "found-space" options, see pages 76–79. An office can also stand alone—for example, consider an armoire (see page 75) or another freestanding furniture piece with doors and drawers.

An upstairs hall can be more than just a passageway, as this 4-foot-wide homework station shows.

A tall, gable-end wall is meticulously fitted with built-in office shelves and cabinets in elegant, dark-stained wood. Traditional cabinetry steps down to the lowered desk surface and back up to tall, shallow bookcases. A sliding ladder (the rail is visible toward the top of the shelves) allows access to upper shelves.

Two drawer units and a file cabinet are bridged by a granite countertop to make a handsome desk. The shallow, white, wall-mounted uppers include recycled windows as glass doors. Integral ceiling moldings link wall unit to room.

A compact office on an upper landing includes sleek, clean-lined wall units that mix open storage and display with sliding doors on discreet hardware. Frosted doors allow a glimpse of what's inside, but hide clutter.

Recessed, glass-doored library cases, crafted in hardwood with brass accents, form a classic backdrop for a formal, wood-paneled study.

Tailored fir built-ins wrap this home office in style. Floor-to-ceiling units, tied together with integral crown and base moldings, include plenty of closed storage below and adjustable shelving above. Along the way there's an efficient built-in desk, plus a comfy looking couch for napping until inspiration strikes.

great wall systems

A recessed wall cabinet or pantry door can provide bonus space for a message center. The unit shown below packs lower drawers, central cubbies, a writing surface, and an upper compartment with a door into one super-slim package.

Tucked in beside the refrigerator, this compact command center includes maple storage niches, black-stained ash drawers, and a cantilevered, angled maple work surface reminiscent of a country school desk.

A kitchen storage wall includes a mini-office, shown above, plus pantry, washer and dryer, and water heater—all tucked behind a series of sliding doors.

What do you do when a home office meets a media center? The handsome cabinetry above features low pullout drawers for heavy vinyl LPs, solid doors for the TV, a countertop for a turntable that needs a lot of vertical space, and glass-fronted uppers for other components.

This efficient armoire adds work space to a bedroom while allowing its owner and designer to put a lid on the workday when it's over. The laminate-lined piece houses a computer, TV, audio gear, work counter, task lights, and storage files—and it's fully wired for action.

found-space solutions

LOOKING FOR STORAGE spaces in all the wrong places? Try some of the following spots: hallways and stairs, entries and exits, unused room corners, closets, and odd nooks and crannies both high and low.

Stairways are prime targets for both storage and display built-ins. The space below stairs is often just waiting to be used; other possibilities include landings as well as stairside shelves or display niches along the way.

In hallways, try between-stud spaces, an open end wall, or look overhead. While you're looking up, check out the soffit areas above kitchen wall cabinets, or kneel down and add drawers or display cubbies below a window seat or island. An angled corner unit can transform any unused corner into a brand-new focal point.

Underutilized closets, if there is such a thing, make ready-made recesses for wall systems; just remove the doors and add shelves. Or borrow the space from a closet in an adjacent room for a built-in unit on the other side.

Some great ideas are even smaller in scale: think pullouts and pantry packs. Modular showrooms and specialty firms have lots of clever accessories you can build in; for shopping tips, see pages 118–121. The ultimate pullout—the Murphy bed—is perfect for guest-room/office multitasking.

Display space is where you find it: in this case, it's tucked into one end of a central kitchen island that is framed in the room's entry.

If your book collection outgrows its allotted space, try breaking it up. This library spreads around a remodeled stair landing leading to the master bedroom. Built-ins along the landing form an intimate book nook where one can study, browse, or simply gaze out through the peaked window wall to greenery beyond.

Perhaps the ultimate found-space retreat, this is more than a window seat:

it's a self-contained nook that functions as a mini-library (note the

bookshelves), a cozy reading nook, a storage chest, and even a guest bed.

While the wedge below the stairs is one way to go, what about the bottoms of the stairs themselves? In this case, the space remains open, but a clever set of ascending shelf niches mirrors the course of the stairs above.

Frustrated by a lack of closets, the owner found space under the staircase in the entry. Two small storage units slide out like drawers, making items immediately and fully accessible. One unit has a seating area for removing shoes; the other holds coats and boots.

Another stairside spot to consider is the wall flanking the stairs' run, often a good opportunity for shallow or recessed shelves. Note how neatly this dark-stained bookcase meets the surrounding plaster.

*What appear to be two simple white cabinet doors (above)
are actually part of a single panel that hides a Murphy bed
(right). These disappearing acts work particularly well in
rooms that serve multiple functions, such as
guest room/home office combinations.*

A freestanding armoire not only invades the kitchen, but the dishwasher is cleverly tucked into its lower left-hand reaches. Most dishwashers accommodate removable, replaceable door panels; in this case, the panel blends seamlessly with the armoire.

One classic spot to tuck display shelves is in the space between vertical wall studs. This narrow, shallow space—typically about 14½ inches wide by 4 inches deep—may be all you need in a hallway, entryway, or bath. As an added benefit, you won't waste any floor space.

Stumped for shelf space? Look up! The kitchen at left did a high-wire act in the so-called "soffit area" atop the door and window trim, which is usually wasted space.

great wall systems

utility players

LAST, BUT NOT LEAST, come those sometimes no-frills wall systems designed for combat duty in places like mudrooms, basements, laundry rooms, workshops, and garages. Typically, these units aren't glamorous, but they're nevertheless important. Think strong materials, easy cleaning, and durability. Also be sure there's good ventilation for stored items.

Bins and baskets may be all you need. For easier access, put them on rollers. Modular budget units abound, with many systems combining closed cabinets, utility shelves, drawers, hooks and rods, and even work counters in one. Sturdy warehouse shelves are another option; combine them with garage pegboard hangers and you're in business. Heavy-duty "ventilated" shelves—typically washable, vinyl-coated steel—perch atop oversize track-and-bracket hardware (see page 90) specially designed for this use. They're great for laundry areas.

A built-in wall unit is one of the best ways to organize a family's sports gear, hats, jackets, shoes, pool towels, and the like.

Modular units range from modest to high-end. This stylish, beautifully made closet system takes the prize for both looks and efficiency. Plenty of drawers, pullouts, clothes rods, and even a swing-down rack at center can allow you to mix and match the system of your dreams.

Don't forget closets. There's an exploding array of stock, custom, and modular units now available. As you'll see, some of these custom or commercial units are not only amazingly efficient; they're also quite stylish.

Store items that are seldom used or dangerous to children on high shelves or inside locked cabinets, small items that are hard to spot at eye level, and light but large items on bottom shelves. Pullouts or pantry packs can help you avoid stooping and can maximize your usable space.

The mud room shown above, an entry alcove located near both laundry room and kitchen, has plenty of nooks and crannies for clothes, ski boots, artwork, and messages. Each family member has his or her own "zone."

In this garage, storage is open—the workhorses are "ventilated" wire shelves on a heavy-duty track-and-bracket system that's designed for utility use and abuse. Another star performer is the wire-basket system that rolls around the space as needed.

The linen closet pictured at left hides maximum shelf space behind a pair of stylish bi-fold doors. The kick base keeps dust from rolling right into the closet and makes cleaning easier.

Wine storage calls not only for stable temperatures, but also for stable shelves and bins. The reason for both notched rails and diamond-shaped bins: wine bottles are expensive, fragile, and—most importantly—round.

Located off the basement hall, this ultimate laundry room contains built-in cabinetry that camouflages storage—as well as both the washer and dryer.

A SHOPPER'S GUIDE

IT'S TIME FOR A SHOPPING SPREE.
Whether you're looking for track-and-bracket shelf hardware, an unfinished armoire, or an ultra-smooth TV pullout, we'll show you shopping options from A to Z (actually, from shelves to moldings) on the following pages. **WE BEGIN WITH THE BASICS**—prefab shelves, shelf materials, and both fixed and adjustable hardware. **THEN IT'S ON TO CABINETS,** doors and drawers, freestanding furniture pieces, and the latest looks in both budget-minded and high-end modular systems. Along the way you'll find lots of specialized pullouts and hardware to make your hardworking wall system work even harder. **FINISHING TOUCHES** include built-in light fixtures; stains, paints, and clear finishes; and stylish moldings that will turn your new unit into an integral part of your home's design.

Shelves

FROM BOARDS AND BRACKETS TO BOOKCASES

Of all storage and display components, shelves are the most basic. They're installed in cabinets, built into all types of wall units, or simply mounted by themselves on brackets or other supports. Some are fixed in place; others are adjustable; still others pull out, swivel, or lift up.

Shelf materials

When you shop, you'll discover shelves made of a variety of materials, including numerous kinds of solid wood, sheet products, and glass. Which is best? That depends on the appearance and strength you want the shelving to have.

Some materials can span farther than others without bowing or breaking under a given load; guidelines are given in the chart on page 16. Use the

CLEAR FIR

maximum spans for lightweight to medium-weight loads, such as art objects, most books, pictures, and relatively lightweight electronic gear. For heavier loads, such as televisions, wine racks, heavy books, and magazine stacks, shorten the spans or use stronger materials. Place only lightweight objects on glass shelving.

PINE, FIR, AND OTHER SOFT-WOODS. Sold as boards through home centers and lumber dealers, these softwoods are favored for relatively inexpensive, do-it-yourself shelving.

Several grades are available. For most shelving, the appearance grades of Select (sometimes called Clear) and Common are preferred. Look for C-and-better Selects if you want flawless, knotless wood. Other less-expensive choices for shelving are No. 2 and No. 3 Common "knotty" pine. Whatever the grade, let your eyes be the final judge.

Boards are sold by the foot, usually in "1-by" (or ¾-inch) thickness, although thicker boards are sometimes available.

"KNOTTY" PINE

Lumberyards will sometimes cut them to length for you. If your boards require finishing, see pages 122–123 for information.

SOLID HARDWOODS. Hardwoods such as oak, cherry, and maple are available through hardwood lumber dealers and some home centers. They're typically available in ⁴⁄₄, ⁵⁄₄, ⁶⁄₄, and ⁸⁄₄ thicknesses—about ¾-inch to 1½ inches. Hardwoods tend to be expensive, particularly in the rare, wide boards required for shelving. (Several widths are often glued together by cabinetmakers—or some home-improvement centers—to form wider boards.)

SHEET PRODUCTS. Hardwood-veneered plywood is more commonly used for shelving than solid hardwood. Plywood is considerably less expensive, comes in wide (4- by 8-foot)

RED OAK

sheets, and won't warp or twist as readily as solid wood. In shelf construction, the plywood is usually edged with hardwood veneer tape (see below) or trimmed with solid hardwood. Other edge treatments are also available.

Particleboard shelves are serviceable but fairly weak; don't pick them for heavy loads. Medium-density fiberboard, or MDF, is stronger than standard fiberboard and is sometimes available in thicker 1-inch pieces. MDF takes paint very well and can be

GLASS SHELF KIT

shaped easily with a router. Though both particleboard and MDF come in 4- by 8-foot sheets, they're also available precut in shelf sizes at home centers.

Shelves covered with vinyl, melamine, plastic laminate, or related films are easy to maintain and relatively inexpensive. Of the three surfacing materials, plastic laminate is by far the most durable. Melamine, a surface layer of resin-impregnated paper, is very serviceable and considerably less expensive than plastic laminate. Vinyl-wrapped shelves are the lowest grade.

GLASS. Plate glass with ground edges is a popular shelf material for displays because it allows you to view objects more fully and doesn't block the light. Choose $\frac{1}{4}$-, $\frac{3}{8}$-, or $\frac{1}{2}$-inch thickness, depending on the span. Some glass suppliers offer a range of colors and surface textures. Though pricier, it's best to opt for tempered safety glass.

VINYL WRAP

PARTICLEBOARD

Other units a designed to be s other. Sometime available in sing triple-length ve nest pieces toge and shape you v

HARDWARE. shelves, shelvin have their own options.

Spade pins a page), made of drilled holes in you to change a

Track-and-c is designed for frames, simplif bookcases and adjust the shelv length, as need in place along more finished l

VENEER TAPE

PAINT-GRADE POPLAR

MELAMINE

Doors and Drawers

LIDS, BOXES, HINGES, AND OTHER HARDWARE

Doors hide clutter, seal out dust, and enliven the appearance of both bookcases and cabinets. Drawers are essentially boxes, that slide in and out. Add doors, drawers, or both to your shelving unit, and you have a full-fledged wall system.

Door details

Cabinet doors can hinge, slide, drop down, fold up, or retract. The type that works best on a particular unit depends on the purpose.

Hinged doors, by far the most common, open easily and allow total access to a cabinet's contents. Sliding doors always look tidy and don't require room to swing, but they allow access into only half the cabinet at a time.

Drop-down doors, which swing down rather than to the side, can double as a work surface.

Folding and tambour (roll-away) doors open the cabinet completely; they require little or no swinging room, but they are sometimes awkward to operate.

Retractable (or "flipper") doors hinge open and then slide back into a cabinet. These doors are particularly effective where hinged doors would be an obstruction. They can be installed either vertically or horizontally.

RETRACTABLE DOORS

SLIDING DOORS

DOUBLE-HINGED
RETRACTABLE DOOR

DROP-DOWN DOOR

Shel

Supp
of yo
uprig
a she
and
at a

RAISED PANEL DOOR

FLAT LAMINATE DOOR

FRAME-AND-PANEL DOOR

FRAMED DECORATIVE GLASS DOOR

FLAT PLYWOOD DOOR

GLASS DOOR

Study cabinet doors and you'll notice that there are several ways to mount a door with respect to the cabinet face. A *recessed* door is mounted inside the opening, with its face flush with the front of the cabinet or face frame. On a *lipped* door, a rabbet (notch) is cut around the inside edges of the door so that half its thickness projects beyond the face frame. An *overlay* door overlaps the edges of the opening and is mounted with its inside face against the cabinet frame.

How doors are made

Cabinet doors are constructed either as flat pieces or as a panel surrounded by a frame. The flat type (shown above) is normally wood veneer or laminate over a core of plywood, particleboard, or medium-density fiberboard (MDF). A frame-and-panel door may be made of solid hardwood or a combination of hardwood frame and veneered panels. The best frames have mortise-and-tenon or doweled joints. Panels may

be flat, veneered sheet products, or shaped or "raised" from solid wood or MDF.

Glass doors, especially those made of etched, beveled, or leaded glass, may utilize a hardwood frame, much like a frame-and-panel door, except that glass replaces the panel. Or glass sheets can be fitted into tracks to serve as sliders. Still other glass doors are hinged; some hinges clamp in place, while others are secured through holes bored in the glass.

Hinges and hardware

Shown on this page is a sampling of the many hinges available to hang different types of doors.

European cup hinges, which are hidden behind the door, are by far the most popular for frameless cabinets and modular wall systems. The best of these are adjustable and allow a door to open completely—110°, 120°, or even 170°—rather than restricting it to a 90° swing. Good European hinges can be aligned simply with a screwdriver; clip-on versions allow you to take the door off and on without touching a screw.

EUROPEAN CUP HINGE

These hinges come in full-overlay, half-overlay, and recessed versions.

Use other hinges for visual impact or special effects. Small butt hinges are traditional for standard face-frame cabinets (see page 112) or other period styles. Other options for standard doors include pin hinges, concealed hinges, and offset hinges (the last for lipped doors only). All these hinges are harder to install and adjust than cup hinges.

Specialty doors have their own hinge styles. Lightweight sliding doors run in wood, metal, or vinyl tracks; heavy sliding doors hang from overhead tracks and runners. Drop-down doors use piano hinges, butterfly hinges, or stay supports to keep them in check; retractable or "flipper" hinges (see page 108) allow doors to fold back completely out of the way. So-called "snap-closing" cup hinges are enough to keep doors closed, but other hinges

may call for catches and latches (see the facing page). Magnetic catches are generally your best bet; they are less dependent on strict alignment than other types and don't wear out. Other alternatives include friction catches, touch latches, and security latches. All these styles are shown on the facing page.

CONCEALED HINGE

GLASS DOOR HINGE

BUTT HINGE

OFFSET HINGE

DECORATIVE BRASS HINGE

STAY SUPPORT

BUTTERFLY HINGE

PIANO HINGE

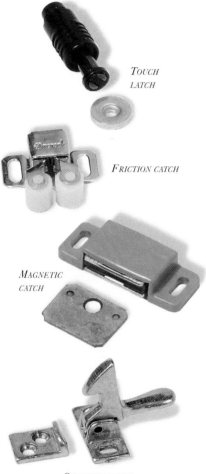

TOUCH LATCH

FRICTION CATCH

MAGNETIC CATCH

SECURITY LATCH

Locks can be used on display cabinets to keep valuables visible but safe. Traditional mortise lock assemblies include a bolt, a strike plate, and an escutcheon, which encircles the keyhole. Cam locks are trimmer, but less secure. If you have more than one lock, you can buy them keyed alike.

CAM LOCK

FINDING THE RIGHT KNOBS AND PULLS

Door and drawer hardware goes a long way toward customizing the look of your unit, both defining style and adding pizzazz.

An endless array of knobs and pulls is available, and you should be able to find something to suit the style of any project. Some screw on, and some bolt through the door or drawer. Flush knobs (designed for sliding doors) and flush pulls must be mounted in holes or mortises. For some projects, a simple hole will make a handsome, serviceable pull.

Make sure you have screws or bolts of the right length to run through your door frame or drawer front. Some bolts are designed to be easily cut to length; if not, try exchanging them for the right fasteners at the hardware store.

Drawer construction

A drawer is essentially a box with four sides and a bottom. The manner in which the box is built is a good way to judge the overall quality of the system. Traditionally, the best drawers have hardwood sides dovetailed to a front panel that is separate from the drawer's face (see above left). A sturdy ¼-inch plywood bottom is set into dadoes, or grooves, in the sides and front, and sometimes in the back. Other high-quality drawers feature void-free marine plywood—called Finnish ply or Apply ply—which has handsome edge detailing and is actually more stable than hardwood.

VINYL-WRAPPED
PARTICLEBOARD

Medium-grade drawers may have sides built of hardwood, standard hardwood plywood, or melamine-surfaced plywood or particleboard. Sides may be doweled and glued, biscuit-joined, secured with knock-down fasteners, or rabbeted (notched) and nailed to front panels.

FINNISH PLYSIDES

Other medium-grade drawers are molded completely from rigid plastics and given a front panel that matches the cabinet system. These drawers are sturdy and maintenance-free.

MELAMINE

Lowest-quality drawers are built of particleboard wrapped with vinyl paper. Some are "folded" together from a single piece and mitered at the corners. Sides are attached directly to the finish front with hot-melt glue and staples, an unreliable method that may result in the drawer's falling apart with time. The bottom is often made of thin, 3/16-inch hardboard.

Like doors, drawer faces can overlay the front frame, sit partially inside the frame, or they can be recessed fully inside the frame.

All about drawer guides

Traditional furniture drawers were simply friction-fit or operated on waxed runners. But furniture aesthetics aside, adding a sturdy set of drawer guides is the best way to go. Side-mounted guides generally handle more weight and operate more smoothly than center guides. These guides require about 1/2-inch clearance between each drawer side and the cabinet frame.

Epoxy-coated, side-mounted, steel slides with nylon rollers (below right) are industry standards, combining easy operation with modest cost. When rollers are rimmed with a rubber ring, action will be smoothest. One nice feature with some of these rollers is that they are self-closing; as the drawer face approaches the cabinet front, it

automatically slides "downhill" into a closed position.

Heavy-duty, steel ball-bearing guides (below left) are stronger and run more smoothly, but they are significantly more expensive. When you push the drawer closed, these guides will seat the drawer firmly against the cabinet front.

Center guides are most appropriate for lightweight, narrow drawers. Some new center guides, though, are stronger, and because they're "invisible," they allow you to combine a guideless, furniture-like appearance with the practicality of a smooth slide.

DRAWER ORGANIZER

(These guides do require substantial bottom clearance.)

The length that guides extend is important to consider, particularly if you'll need full access to the backs of drawers. Most drawer guides extend only three-quarters of their length; high-quality ball-bearing guides extend completely. Most good guide designs allow the drawer to be disconnected and removed from the cabinet.

CUSTOM CORNER DRAWER

EPOXY-COATED SLIDE

HEAVY-DUTY BALL-BEARING GUIDE

Storage Furniture

THESE STAND-ALONES WERE THE FIRST WALL SYSTEMS

Loosely speaking, the term "furniture" means movable—a unit that's either freestanding or attached to a wall for support. Beyond that, furniture implies "tradition," although not all furniture-like wall systems look traditional. These days they range from country casual to formal elegance. In general, furniture units are ready-made and available on short notice. You'll wait longer to have custom furniture designed and/or built by a woodworking professional.

UNFINISHED ARMOIRE

UNFINISHED BOOKCASE

With a few exceptions, furniture designs are not as flexible as modular wall systems (see pages 104–107). Still, a visit to a retail furniture showroom will unveil a surprising range of ready-made storage and display options. You'll discover budget bookcases, Shaker-style media centers, French etageres, and many styles of chests and cabinets that can be used individually or in groupings to meet your display and storage needs.

Storage pieces

Stand-alone furniture pieces are fun to find and are especially apt for eclectic or country-style decorating schemes. Buy them new, buy them as antiques, or rescue them from thrift shops. Or look for unfinished pieces and put your personal stamp on them, saving money in the process.

Bookcases run the gamut from particleboard and pine boards to fine hardwoods like walnut and cherry. Some have bare-bones styling; others sport ornate moldings and face frames (see page 112). Do you need adjustable shelves or extra-deep or extra-strong spans? You're sure to find a bookcase to meet any budget.

Armoires are tall, capacious cupboards with doors and sometimes drawers. Depending on how you outfit them inside, they can fulfill their traditional purpose as clothes closets or house anything from office supplies to your audiovisual equipment.

Hutches and other wood cabinets have been made in a seemingly limitless variety of sizes and types, from wall and corner cupboards to dry sinks, pie safes, and chests of drawers. The classic choice for storing dishes and glassware, a hutch can just as easily become a display case for sculpture or a collection.

Also be on the lookout for roll-top desks, trunks, chests, china cabinets, and buffets.

ANTIQUE HUTCH

TANSU CHEST

CUSTOM CONTEMPORARY PIECE

*HANDPAINTED
CUPBOARD*

Furniture collections

Many large furniture manufacturers offer collections of furniture—as many as twenty or so pieces—designed to coordinate in style and finish. Most collections include specialized pieces such as media centers, china cabinets, and storage units.

Some storage furnishings come as a single piece, such as the tall armoire. Others consist of cabinets or units that you stack up or join side by side. Perhaps the oldest example of the stacked type is the lowboy with a highboy deck. Another example is the china deck that sits on top of a credenza.

Side-by-side groupings generally include different types of tall cabinets. For example, you can buy a tall curio cabinet as a center piece, add matching pier cabinets on either side of it, and finish off the ends with angled corner units. The result is a coordinated wall of cabinetry suited to a variety of purposes. These ensembles were, in fact, the original "wall systems."

Where can you buy it?

You can buy storage furniture at many outlets, including furniture stores, department stores, and designer showrooms. Some single pieces are sold through mail-order catalogs. For complete media centers or furniture to organize electronic gear, visit quality home-electronics stores. And if you look around a bit, you can find ready-made storage solutions in many other places, among them antique stores, unfinished furniture stores, and office-supply outlets.

As a rule, furniture stores excel in service. Many offer design help, financing, and, if needed, assembly.

*DESK GROUPING
(OPEN AND CLOSED)*

KITCHEN HUTCH WITH "DISTRESSED" FINISH

Most department stores sell from floor models or catalogs. They offer the same services as furniture stores, but, because floor space is limited, you may not find as large a selection. Department stores buy mostly from large, established manufacturers.

Designer showrooms sell ready-made and custom storage furniture and wall systems at wholesale prices to designers and architects. To view products in these showrooms and to make purchases, you may need to be accompanied by a professional.

Judging quality

As with any furniture, quality is often self-evident in the appearance and materials of a product. The best pieces are made of durable, high-grade materials such as solid hardwood and/or hardwood plywood. The quality of the piece is generally reflected in the joinery and detailing of doors, drawers, and similar parts (see pages 94–99).

Of course, the higher the quality, the higher the price.

Modular Wall Systems

MIX AND MATCH YOUR FAVORITE PIECES

Born in Scandinavia, modular wall systems have over the years gained favor worldwide as sensible, practical, and sometimes beautiful display and storage units.

It's easy to understand the appeal of a modular system. The keys to its success are modular design, functional flexibility, and ease of installation. You can combine shelves, cabinets, doors, drawers, and other components to fit your exact needs and space requirements. And, when you move, you simply pack up the pieces and take them with you and rearrange them for your new situation.

Most manufacturers offer scores of components, accessories, and finishes. One company produces more than 200 different components and accessories in three kinds of wood and more than two dozen finishes, with seven kinds of hardware. At the very least, nearly

32-MILLIMETER HOLES

all systems are sold in a range of heights, widths, and depths.

Components often include several types of cabinets, a variety of shelves, several different doors, desk units, drawers, integral bases, light fixtures, even fold-up beds. In addition, many

systems offer a range of special accessories, such as CD racks, swiveling pullout television shelves, wine racks, and other helpful organizers. (For more about these special components and accessories, see pages 118–121.)

Despite this diversity, practically all systems allow you to combine differing components and accessories into one integrated unit, enabling you to create custom-looking pieces of furniture at stock prices. One way manufacturers do this is by configuring their components on a 32-millimeter grid, meaning that uprights are drilled every 32 millimeters to receive hinges, shelf pegs, drawer guides, fasteners, and other hardware.

Preassembled or RTA?

Some modular systems are largely preassembled; all you need to do is mount the components on supports. With other systems, you may need to install door fronts on cabinets; still others require that you assemble everything, even the drawers.

This last type (units that come completely disassembled and packed flat in boxes) is referred to as "ready-to-assemble," or RTA. Manufacturers of such systems avoid assembly labor costs and high shipping expenses, passing the savings along to you in exchange for (hopefully!) only a few hours of your time.

Most RTA storage systems are made of melamine, laminate, or wood-

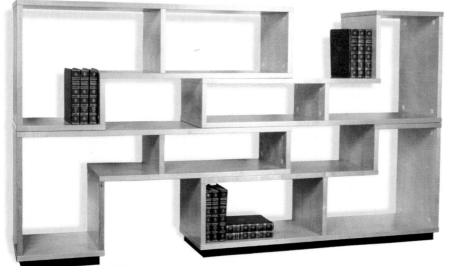

BOOKCASE MODS

STACKABLE MODS

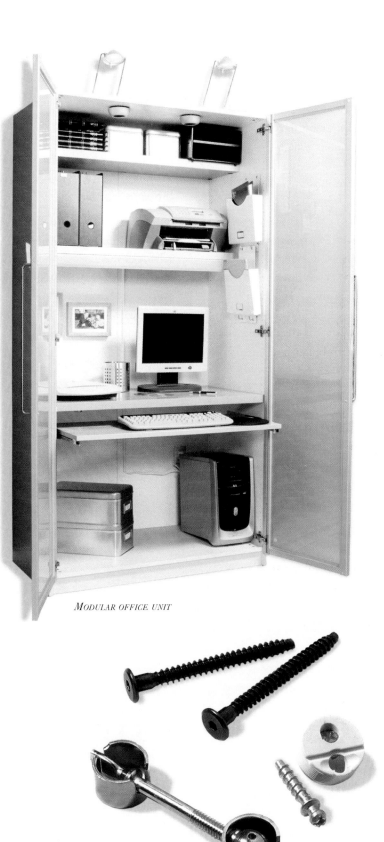

MODULAR OFFICE UNIT

veneered panels that are connected with special "knockdown" (KD) hardware. Two types of knockdown hardware are available. One type allows you to disassemble the components for storage or transport; the other joins pieces permanently. Some common KD fittings are shown at right.

Assembly is usually a straightforward job, requiring a few basic hand tools, sometimes included in the package.

Remember, however, that modules can be extremely heavy when they're fully assembled; you may need a helper or two. Also, some finished units are so large that they will need to be constructed on-site, in the room where they'll be located.

KNOCKDOWN (KD)
HARDWARE

Where to buy them

These days, modular wall systems are showing up in lots of places at a variety of prices. You'll still find many of the best-quality, most flexible, and most attractive units at high-end specialty stores. Showroom personnel in these stores, as well as the people at retailers featuring European designs, work with you to figure your exact needs.

What's new is that there's a rapidly expanding, wider range of less expensive furniture shown at home warehouses and office-supply stores or on the pages of mail-order storage catalogs. You won't find top materials or styles here—or much service—but if your needs are modest and well defined, these sources might be just the ticket.

The modular idea is even migrating to home-improvement centers in the form of budget-minded utility units. For a closer look, see pages 114–115.

Judging quality

Wall system quality is partly a matter of materials, fit, and available components. It's also a matter of looks. You could spend $100 to $10,000; the trick is to buy what's appropriate for your needs and your budget.

Most lower-end units are built from particleboard covered with vinyl-wrapped veneers or laminate. Sometimes you'll find solid pine or relatively soft, less-desirable hardwoods like alder or aspen.

Better lines feature stronger MDF (medium-density fiberboard) cores,

EUROPEAN WALL SYSTEM (OPEN AND CLOSED)

DISPLAY WALL WITH SLIDING DOORS
AND LIBRARY LADDER

either ¾-inch or 1-inch thick, and better veneers—real wood or high-quality laminates with woodlike texture. Some lines offer solid-wood doors and drawer faces in classic hardwood species like maple and cherry. Wood units are finished with subtle, durable layers of penetrating oil, lacquer, or varnish (see pages 122–123).

When shopping, keep the following questions in mind:

- What components, widths, depths, and heights are available? What finishes? What accessories?

- How much design help can you expect?

- Is installation included or available for a fee?

- What sort of guarantee comes with the unit?

- How easy is the system to assemble (if necessary), and how easy to move and reassemble? Are the joints strong enough, and/or are knockdown fasteners up to the task of repeated use?

- How is the unit secured to the wall? Are leveling feet included?

Media Centers

CORRAL TVS, CDS, AND SURROUND-SOUND SYSTEMS

Televisions, audiovisual receivers, DVD players, surround-sound speakers, compact disc collections—where does it all go? Fortunately, wall system manufacturers are becoming attentive to this problem, and there's an entire new generation of media cabinets and organizers out there. We'll outline your options below. Need help planning for electronics? See pages 18–21.

When shopping for media cabinets, some general questions to ask include: Can the unit handle the size and weight of all your components? Is there room for expansion? How will wires enter and exit? What about ventilation and air circulation? Do you need protection from dust?

TV solutions

They're big, they're wide, and they're bulky. Large-screen televisions are posing new challenges for both wall systems and stand-alone storage units.

Television stands come in solid pine, metal, melamine, and laminate; with or without wheels; and with or without a swiveling top. Many have drawers and DVD compartments behind glass doors. Some electronics companies make integral bases that echo the design of their television sets. These bare-bones, mundane-looking platforms sit on the floor, with the TV perching on top.

You'll also discover a growing number of pullouts and turntables for TVs (some products include both), and even lifts that raise the television up from a wall cabinet below. Order these from a wall-system dealer or buy the hardware and fit it to your own cabinetry. For a closer look at cabinet accessories, see pages 118–121.

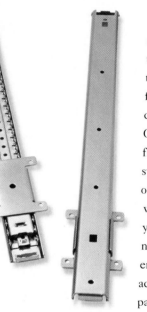

RETRACTABLE "FLIPPER" DOOR HARDWARE

HEAVY-DUTY TV PULLOUT WITH SWIVELING TOP

BALL-BEARING TURNTABLE

Rack 'em up

The now-traditional solution for audio components, so-called "racks," allows you to stack components vertically and access them from either the front or back. Most racks resemble vertical shelving units, with frames and shelves built from laminate or metal. For dust protection, most have fronts (and sometimes tops) of hinged glass or acrylic. Some units have backs as well. Many racks roll on wheels, a handy feature unless you have plush carpeting.

Make sure your components will fit side to side and front to back. (Remember that you don't simply need room for the components, you need extra depth—at least 2 inches—for the wire connections behind them.)

There's also a trend toward low-lying, horizontal A/V units, featuring side-by-side dividers or a series of stackable, modular cubbyholes. Some TV stands include lower compartments for these units.

Thinking low-tech? Simple solutions include open shelves and shelving units (see pages 88–93)—just be sure they're deep enough for the task at hand.

Shop for racks at mass-market electronics stores or see audio specialists. Or check out home-furnishing and storage catalogs.

ENTERTAINMENT ARMOIRE

MOBILE TV CART

MODULAR ENTERTAINMENT UNIT

*INTEGRAL HOME
THEATER SYSTEM*

Moving up to home theater

Some home theater setups are basically a large-screen TV and a DVD player. Others include an A/V receiver, six or more speakers, the audio components discussed above, and more. If all of these components are grouped together, the big systems obviously call for different setups than we've talked about so far.

Small-scale media cabinets, capable of housing television and audio gear

and related items, are available as pre-assembled furniture or knockdown, ready-to-assemble kits. Materials range from solid pine, oak, and alder to veneered particleboard and MDF panels.

Entertainment armoires are also available in a number of styles and finishes. Look for retractable "flipper" doors or those that fold back on double hinges. Be sure TV pullouts or turntables can handle the weight of your

equipment. Drawers are a must for organizing the small stuff.

On a slightly larger scale, say enough room for a large TV, A/V receiver, and three front surround-sound speakers, look to furniture stores, mass-market electronics stores, or wall system specialists. Or assemble stock base and wall cabinets (pages 112–113) under a countertop.

For full-blown media centers, your best bets are furniture ensembles, large modular wall systems, or custom cabinetry from a cabinetmaker or fabricator who works with audiovisual consultants. Materials for custom units typically are hardwood plywood, solid hardwood, or MDF. As to price, the sky's the limit.

*CABINET
FAN*

*HARDWOOD VENT
GRILLE*

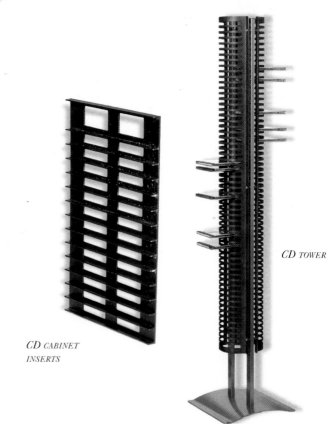

CD ORGANIZER

CD TOWER

CD CABINET INSERTS

Combating chaos

Compact discs, DVDs, vintage vinyl, and other media collections get out of hand quickly, but there's help available. Prefabricated cubes, towers, and wall units are one solution. Or buy grooved CD inserts, shown at right, and use them to line a bookcase or drawer.

Snarls of electrical wires and cables are another form of creeping chaos. To control the snarl, see "Tame Those Wires," below.

TAME THOSE WIRES

Forget the paper-free revolution—how about a cord-free revolution? Between TVs, DVD players, surround-sound speakers, computers, and a swarm of phone lines, wires can create a real Gordian knot around and behind your wall system.

Fortunately, a new generation of wire-management devices, several of which are pictured at right, now comes to the rescue.

Desktop grommets, round or oblong and available in numerous sizes and finishes, are probably the easiest aids to find. Troughs direct cords along the back of a desk to a point where they can all exit. Vertical channels direct wires to the floor and match some troughs. Friction clips hold wires tight to the desk like brooms in a broom closet. Raceways mount to desk, wall, or floor and direct wires any-where. Surge protectors not only guard against power spikes but help organize your cords.

Grommets, raceways, and troughs are showing up at some office-supply, computer, and hardware stores; otherwise, try office outlets or woodworking mail-order sources. You'll find wire ties, wire staples, plastic conduit, and other hardware at electrical-supply houses and in the electrical departments of some home-improvement centers and hardware stores.

Stock Cabinets

KITCHEN AND BATH UNITS DANCE NEW STEPS

Factory-made cabinets, the type typically used in kitchens and bathrooms, are an important option to consider when you're planning permanent, built-in display or storage for any room in your home.

Sold through cabinet dealers and home-improvement centers, manufactured cabinets come in many styles, from relatively inexpensive stock models to high-end, semi-custom creations. The three main configurations are base, wall, and specialty cabinets. You can gang them side by side or stack them to create storage walls, room dividers, buffets, entertainment centers, and much more.

Traditional or European-style?

First, you'll need to decide whether you want framed or frameless cabinets.

Traditional American cabinets mask the raw front edges of each box with a 1-by-2 "face frame." Doors and drawers then fit in one of three ways: inset within the frame; partially offset, with a lip; or completely overlaying the frame.

Since the face frame covers up the basic box, thinner or lower-quality wood can be used in its sides, somewhat decreasing the cost. But the frame takes up space and reduces the size of the openings, so drawers or slide-out accessories must be significantly smaller than the full width of the cabinet, slightly decreasing storage capacity.

Europeans, when faced with postwar lumber shortages, came up with "frameless" cabinets. A simple trim strip covers raw edges, which butt directly against one another. Doors and drawers often fit to within ⅛-inch of each other, revealing a thin sliver of the trim. Interior components, such as drawers, can be sized almost to the full dimensions of the box.

Another big difference: frameless cabinets typically have a separate toespace pedestal, or plinth, below them. This allows you to set counter heights specifically to your liking, stack base units, or make use of space at floor level.

Basic size options

Cabinets typically are manufactured in sizes from 9 to 48 inches wide, in 3-inch increments.

Base cabinets, typically 34½ inches tall and 24 inches deep, are made to fit under kitchen counters, so they probably won't have a top panel. Wall cabinets measure 12, 18, 24, 30, 48, and 60 inches high; 30 inches wide, and 12 inches deep is standard.

Tall cabinets—often some of the best components for general storage—come 84, 90, and 96 inches high. Wardrobe and hutch-style accessories vary from 30 to 96 inches tall and from 18 to 24 inches deep.

OVERLAY DOORS AND DRAWERS

You can specify door styles, direction of door swing, and whether side panels are finished; sometimes you get other options and add-ons (see pages 118–121).

So-called semi-custom systems come in a wide range of sizes, with many options for each size. If necessary, heights, widths, and depths can be modified to fit almost any design.

Because semi-custom cabinets are configured to order and many are imported from abroad, it may take longer to receive them than it would to order custom units from a local cabinetmaker. Order either type of cabinet as far ahead as possible.

RTA
(READY-TO-ASSEMBLE)
CABINET

Judging quality

To determine the quality of a stock cabinet, first look at the drawers. They take more of a beating than any other part. Several designs are shown on page 98.

Door hinges are also critical hardware elements. European cup hinges (page 96) are the most trouble free type of hinge. They are the best choices unless you want the period look of surface hardware.

Most cabinet boxes are made from sheet products like hardwood plywood, particleboard (plain or laminated), or medium-density fiberboard. If solid lumber is used, it's usually reserved for doors and drawer faces. For a rundown on these products, see pages 12–13.

A recent development, the so-called RTA (ready-to-assemble) cabinet, costs even less than other stock units, but requires some basic tools and elbow grease to put together. An RTA stock cabinet is shown above.

FACE FRAME CABINETS

FRAMELESS CABINETS

Utility Units

THEY'RE STURDY—AND EVEN STYLISH

Closets, laundry rooms, pantries, basements, and garages—sometimes these spaces get no respect, but they can still gain valuable display and storage space via wall systems and shelving. These specialized offerings, which we might call utility units, range from the truly prosaic to those that rival the looks of a living room's most stylish displays.

Buying the basics

Some utility units are beautiful, others simply inexpensive. You'll find a selection of serviceable, budget-minded closet and garage lines at home centers. These systems follow the same modular principle as the more stylized European wall systems (see pages 104–107). A certain number of interchangeable boxes, rods, shelves, drawer units, and countertops can be mixed and matched to form a system that works for you. Most of these units are made from particleboard, some with melamine (a better choice) or vinyl veneers on top. Both painted and plastic versions are available.

The home-center units are typically packed flat, RTA-style. You load the boxes (which can be heavy), take them home, and assemble them. Some dealers will deliver and install for a fee.

In addition to modular boxes, you'll also find open-wire or "ventilated" shelf systems. These systems are popular for use in closets, dressing rooms, laundries, and pantry areas. Some wire systems are chrome-plated, some are galvanized, and others have a white or black vinyl coating on the wire. Some manufacturers also make pullout wire baskets, wall hooks, and other accessories that can be used alone or mixed with the shelf modules. Support for all this comes from a backing grid (see the facing page), a ladder frame, or some variation on the track-and-bracket scheme (see page 90).

On the garage front, you also have a number of industrial-type options, including pegboard, steel, and plastic shelving units, bare particleboard modules, and units that are built from resin-coated MDF.

When it comes to utility shelves, pay attention to the spans; manufacturers may be overly optimistic about the weights their designs carry. Particleboard, the substratum for most budget units, is unreliable for even medium loads and spans. For more details on shelf spans and reinforcement, see page 16.

VENTILATED UTILITY SHELVES

PEGBOARD AND HOOKS

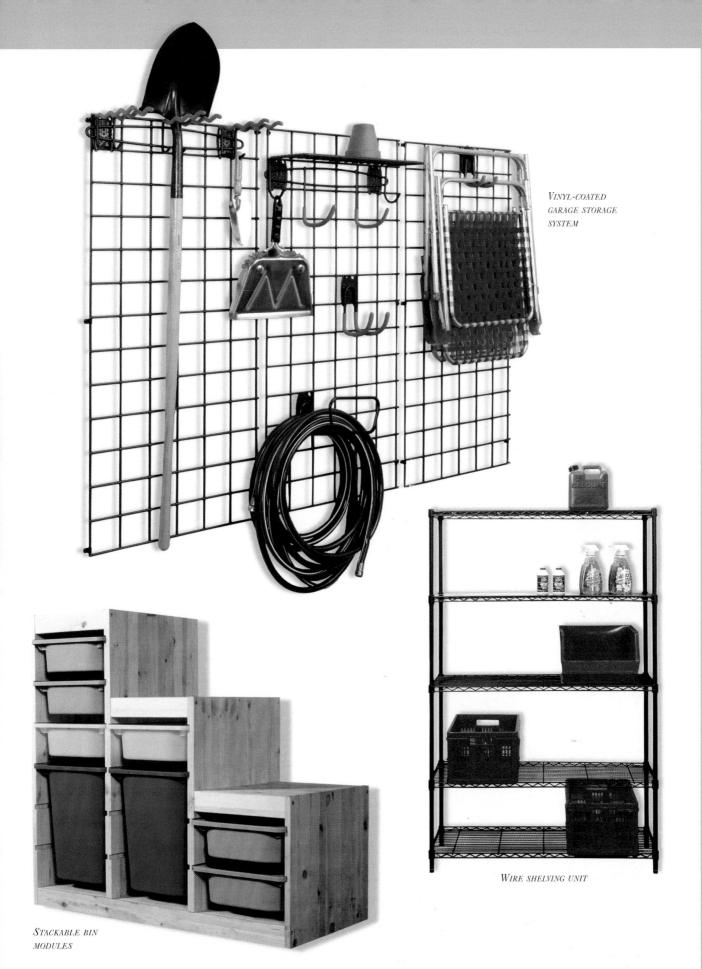

Vinyl-coated garage storage system

Wire shelving unit

Stackable bin modules

"BUILT-IN" CLOSET WITH INTEGRAL ROOM DIVIDER

A step up

Specialty firms offer better looks, better materials, and complete design services—all for a price. To shop, look in the yellow pages under "Closets & Closet Accessories"; most offerings are designed for closets and home offices. Some companies mix and match stock sizes; others will make any size unit you need. Typically, you fill out a questionnaire and provide overall measurements.

Most systems are based on the now-classic 32-millimeter design concept that allows you to plug in doors, drawers, adjustable shelves, closet rods, and other offerings. Units are usually built from particleboard and melamine. Some firms offer laminate veneers and choices of door and drawer styles. Expect prices to rise with options.

Basically, the best units are extensions of higher-end modular systems. Look for MDF or plywood cores, hardwood or laminate veneers, and a range of door and drawer shapes and styles (see pages 94–99), many in solid hardwood. For more shopping pointers, see pages 104–107.

MOVABLE CLOSET CART

MODULAR CLOSET COMPONENTS

Accessories

ADD CUSTOM EFFICIENCY WITH STOCK HARDWARE

Nearly all wall system manufacturers, and a growing number of other companies, offer at least a few special components and accessories that stretch the capabilities of the units. These choices allow you to turn an ordinary wall system into a multifunctional machine by day and then to fold it all up at night.

For example, what appears to be a waist-high drawer may be a drop-down door that reveals a pullout ironing board. Deep drawer fronts can hide roomy hanging-file systems. A breakfast table or desktop can pull straight out of a wall system or fold down into place. A television can magically rise from the top of a cabinet.

You'll find specialty add-ons for every imaginable use: home theater, home office, kitchen, bath, guest room, closet, and garage.

WIRE PULLOUT BINS

FOLD-DOWN CABINET SHELVES

CABINET INSERT ORGANIZERS

FOLD-DOWN TABLE

MEDIA PULLOUT

WIRE OFFICE ORGANIZERS

TRIPLE-EXTENSION WORK COUNTER

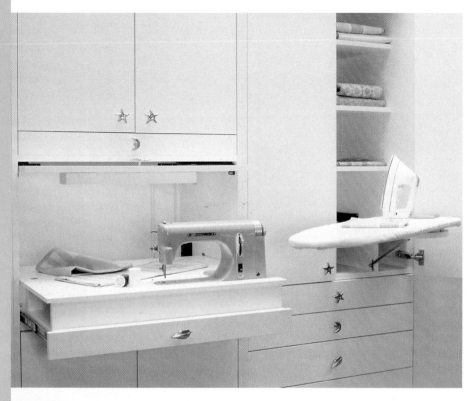

MODULAR
SEWING CENTER

FOLD-DOWN
IRONING BOARD

PULLOUT BINS

PULLOUT
IRONING BOARD

Most fittings for these specialized pieces are produced by European hardware manufacturers. The products are sold directly through catalogs and distributors to cabinet manufacturers, custom woodworking shops, and some well-stocked builder's-hardware retailers. Some lines are now showing up in home centers; others are available via mail-order woodworking and specialty home catalogs and from the Internet.

If you're outfitting a preexisting cabinet or one bought from another source, be sure to check the sizes and clearances required for add-ons; they usually have clearly prescribed tolerances.

*MODULAR MURPHY BED
(OPEN AND CLOSED)*

*MODULAR
HOME GYM*

Finishing Touches

STAINS, TOP COATS, LIGHTS, AND MOLDINGS

Details make the difference between a mundane wall system and a handsome one. To make both room and wall unit appear as an integrated setting, consider three main areas: finish, auxiliary lighting, and moldings.

A fine finish

A wood's finish dramatically affects its impact. But a good finish also keeps dirt and moisture out of wood pores, wards off dents, and protects the wood from abrasion, heat, and chemicals.

Solid wood or wood-veneered wall systems can be treated with any of several types of stains, paints, and clear coatings. The chart on the facing page outlines the characteristics of common wood-finishing products. For additional help, consult your paint dealer.

Both stains and finishes come in traditional oil-base and newer water-base versions. All things being equal, choose the water-base products—they're easier to use, clean up with water, and produce far fewer noxious fumes than the oil-base products.

STAINS. In most cases, stains are not final finishes; they are used for color or accent only. You still need to seal the surface with a clear finish. If your pieces are made of unfinished pine, apply a sealer before staining to achieve even coloring.

Though you may encounter many stain names and brands, products fall

GEL STAIN

PENETRATING OIL

WATER-BASE VARNISH

into two general types: pigmented stains and dyes. Pigmented stains, sold as oil stain, wood stain, and pigmented wiping stain, are composed of finely ground particles of color held in suspension in oil solvent.

Dyes are mostly aniline (a coal-tar derivative), dissolved in either water or alcohol. Because they are actually absorbed by the wood fibers, dye stains allow the grain to show through. If you can't find dyes at retail stores, look for them in wood-finishing specialty stores or woodworking catalogs.

CLEAR FINISHES. Generally, clear finishing products fall into two basic types: penetrating finishes and surface coatings.

Penetrating finishes soak into the pores of the wood to give it a natural look and feel. Though a penetrating finish sinks below the wood's surface, it's still fairly durable—without the "dipped-in-plastic" appearance of

some of the more protective coatings.

Surface finishes lie on top of the wood and provide protection in the form of a thin, durable shield. This kind of coating, often available in a number of sheens, may be glasslike in appearance, but it can be dulled down, if desired, by rubbing.

ENAMELS. Water-base (latex) and oil-base (alkyd) enamels are both used for interior surfaces. Latex paints are easier to use because water is their solvent, but alkyds are more durable.

Paint finishes range from flat, or matte, to high gloss. Since there's no industry standard for sheens, a medium gloss may be called pearl, semi-gloss, or some other name, and it can range from moderately to very shiny, depending on the manufacturer. The glossier the finish, the more durable and washable it is.

A LOOK AT FINISHING PRODUCTS

STAINS

Pigmented oil stain

Simple to apply; won't fade or bleed. Useful for making one wood species look like another. Heavy pigments tend to obscure grain and gum up pores in hardwoods such as oak and walnut. Not compatible with shellac or lacquer.

Penetrating oil stain

One-step product stains with dyes rather than pigments, so pores and grain show through. Similar to penetrating resin, but with color added. Produces irregular results on softwoods and plywoods. Handy for repairs, touch-up jobs.

Gel stain

May contain both pigments and dyes. Very easy to apply (just wipe on, buff out, and let dry), but results may be uneven on large surfaces.

Aniline dye (water base)

Colors are brilliant, clear, and permanent. Since water raises wood grain, light resanding may be necessary. Very slow drying. Sold in powdered form; can be hard to find.

Aniline dye (alcohol base)

Quick-drying alcohol stains won't raise grain, but they aren't very light-fast; they're best reserved for small touch-up jobs. Should be sprayed on to avoid lap marks.

Non-grain-raising stain

Bright, transparent colors; won't raise wood grain. Available premixed by mail. Very short drying time; best when sprayed. Not for use on softwoods.

PENETRATING FINISHES

Boiled linseed oil

Lends warm, slightly dull patina to wood. Dries very slowly and requires many coats. Moderate resistance to heat, water, and chemicals. Easily renewable.

Tung oil

Natural oil finish that's hard and highly resistant to abrasion, moisture, heat, acid, and mildew. Requires several thin, hand-rubbed applications (heavy coats wrinkle badly). Best with polymer resins added.

Penetrating resin (Danish oil, antique oil)

Use on hard, open-grain woods. Leaves wood looking and feeling "natural." Easy to apply and retouch, but doesn't protect against heat or abrasion. May darken some woods.

Rub-on varnish

Penetrating resin and varnish combination that builds up sheen as coats are applied; dries fairly quickly. Moderately resistant to water and alcohol. Darkens wood.

SURFACE FINISHES

Shellac

Lends warm luster to wood. Lays down in thin, quick-drying coats that can be rubbed to a high sheen. Little resistance to heat, alcohol, and moisture. Comes in white (blonde), orange, and brownish (button) versions. Available in flake form or premixed.

Lacquer (nitrocellulose)

Strong, clear, quick-drying finish in both spraying and brushing form. Very durable, though vulnerable to moisture. Requires 3 or more coats; can be polished to a high gloss. Noxious fumes; highly flammable.

Lacquer (water base)

Easier to clean, less toxic, and much less flammable than nitrocellulose lacquer—more practical spray product for do-it-yourselfer. Raises grain; use sanding sealer. May dry more slowly than nitrocellulose lacquer. Can smell strongly of ammonia.

Varnish (oil base)

Widely compatible oil-base interior varnish that produces a thick coating with good overall resistance. Comes in numerous sheens. Dries slowly and darkens with time. Brush marks and dust can be a problem.

Varnish (water base)

Easy cleanup. Dries quickly; nontoxic when dry. Though early versions lacked durability, new products are greatly improved. Finish goes on milky, but dries clear and won't yellow. Raises wood grain. May require numerous coats. Expensive.

Polyurethane varnish

Thick, plastic, irreversible coating that's nearly impervious to water, heat, and alcohol. Dries overnight. Incompatible with some stains and sealers. Follow instructions to ensure good bonding between coats.

Enamel

Available in flat, semigloss, and gloss sheens, and in a wide range of colors. May have lacquer or varnish (alkyd, water, or polyurethane) base; each shares same qualities as clear finish of the same type.

Wax

Occasionally used as a finish, especially on antiques or "aged" pine. More often applied over harder top coats. Increases luster of wood. Not very durable, but offers some protection against liquids when renewed frequently. Available in various shades.

Lighting for shelves

Whether you use wall systems to conceal clutter or display treasures, you should pay attention to one other ingredient—light. With the proper lighting, your wall system becomes not only more functional but also more aesthetically pleasing.

You can light shelves from either inside or outside the unit. If you're building a custom unit, consider adding recessed or indirect lighting during construction. Your basic options include recessed downlights, canisters, track lights, strip lights, and under-cabinet task lights. Commercial wall systems often include light "bridges" (soffits with downlights) or built-ins as accessory options.

Recessed downlights and tracks can be located either at the top of the unit or in the ceiling with light directed down to the unit. Most built-in canisters are low-voltage, meaning they require a transformer to "step down" power from standard household current to a more manageable 12 volts. Why go low voltage? The fixtures are much smaller and they use less energy. Most low-voltage fixtures house either halogen or xenon (a cooler-burning cousin) bulbs.

For high-lighting wall systems, it's usually best to buy swiveling lights or lights that can be aimed at a unit.

Strip lights resemble Christmas tree lights. Some are housed on a flexible backing strip; others, called rope lights, are tucked inside clear or colored plastic tubing. Put strip lights out of sight inside the unit or above the top, shining up to outline the unit. You shouldn't see the bulbs, just the glow.

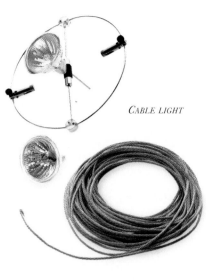

CABLE LIGHT

TRANSFORMER

LOW-VOLTAGE XENON DOWNLIGHT

ROPE LIGHT

Several kinds of under-cabinet fixtures are available: halogen, incandescent, and fluorescent. Most are compatible with standard household current and are available in switched (plug-in) and wire-in (direct-wired) versions. Designed for kitchen counters, they can light a wall system's work surface from above, or they can be mounted inside the top of the cabinet so that light washes down.

A dimmer switch is a big plus for any lighting scheme: it allows you to dial your wall system's lighting up and down as the mood dictates. A pressure switch turns the light on when you open a cabinet door.

Installing cabinet lighting may require the services of an electrician.

Moldings and trim

Even the most basic shelving unit can be dressed up by the addition of moldings. Whether applied to the face of the unit or to the surrounding wall, moldings can add classic detailing and visually integrate the wall system with the rest of the room.

Moldings come in a wide range of standard profiles, including crown molding, baseboard, and window and door casing. You can also buy reproductions of architectural details, such as pediments, mantels, and pilasters. Before you shop, collect ideas by studying how moldings have been used in the wall systems shown in this book. Then browse through a molding dealer's selection to see how different moldings can be combined to form interesting profiles.

You can buy stock moldings from lumberyards or home centers, and special or custom patterns from molding and millwork shops. Priced by the linear foot, they vary widely, from about 15 cents per foot for small, simple patterns to more than $15 per foot for ornate architectural styles. "Paint-grade" pine moldings, which have visible finger joints along their length, are much less expensive than "stain-grade" oak or other hardwoods that can be finished

MOLDINGS

naturally. You can buy moldings either unfinished or coated with primer waiting for you to add the top coats.

If you're painting, also take a look at moldings made from medium-density fiberboard. MDF takes paint very well, is less expensive than most wood moldings, and is less prone to warping than wood—especially in large profiles like crown molding. Most MDF moldings come preprimed.

Though some restoration-quality architectural moldings are still milled from hardwoods, most ornate moldings are now cast from polyurethane and are meant to be painted.

design & photography credits

design

FRONT MATTER

1 Design: Freddy Moran and Carlene Anderson Kitchen Design **5** Interior design: EJ Interior Design, Inc.

A PLANNING PRIMER

6 Architect: Obie Bowman. Styling: Julie Atwood **11 (upper left)** Design: Jane Walter and Robert Adams/Summer-House **11 (upper right)** Ikea **19 (both)** Interior design: Sandy Bacon/Sandy Bacon Design Group. Home theater: John Maxon/Integrated System Design. Cabinets: Heartwood Studio

21 (upper left three and bottom right) Ikea **22** Interior design: David Ramey/David Ramey Interior Design **23 (top)** Interior design: Ann Jones Interiors **24 (bottom left)** Architect: Scott Johnson **25 (top right)** Architect: Mui Ho **25 (bottom left)** Architect: Dave Davis/Dixon Weinstein Architects **25 (bottom right)** Organized Living

GREAT WALL SYSTEMS

26 Architect: Jarvis Architects **28** Architect: David Stark Wilson/Wilson Architects **29** Interior design: Sasha Emerson Design Studio **30 (bottom)** Design: Holly Opfelt Design **31 (top left)** Interior design: City Studios **31 (top right)** The Container Store **31 (bottom)** Pottery Barn **32 (top)** Interior design: Bauer Interior Design **32 (bottom right)** Interior design: Wayne Palmer **33** Design: Nina Bookbinder **34 (top)** Architect: Colleen Mahoney/Mahoney Architects. General contractor: Cove Construction **35** Design: Cheng Design **37** Building design: William Gottlieb. Interior design: Markie Nelson **38** Interior design: Mel Lowrance **39** Design: Terri Taylor **40 (top)** Architect: Steven Goldstein **40 (bottom)** Interior design: EJ Interior design, Inc. **41** Architect: Mark Becker Inc. **42 (top)** Design: Jacobson, Silverstein & Winslow Architects/Paul Winans Construction Inc. **42 (bottom)** Architect/designer: Donald Clement. Cabinet fabrication: Apple Woodworks **43 (top)** Architect/designer: Donald Clement. Cabinet fabrication: Apple Woodworks **43 (bottom)** Interior design: Kit Parmentier/Allison Rose **44** Design: Daniel and Christine Hale/DMH The Art of Furniture **45** Design: Nancy Gilbert/San Anselmo Country Store **46 (top)** Interior design: Janice Olson/JD–Just Design by Janice **46 (bottom)** Interior design: Sasha Emerson Design Studio **47 (bottom right)** Architect: Mark Becker, Interior design: Tami Becker **48** Interior design: Linda Applewhite **49** Architect: Charles Rose. General contractor: Dennis Jones. Lighting designer: Linda Ferry **50 (top)** Architect: Remick Associates Architects-Builders, Inc. Leaded glass window: Masaoka Glass Design **50 (bottom)**

Architect: Edward Buchanan/Jarvis Architects **52** Architect: Charles Rose. General contractor: Dennis Jones. Lighting designer: Linda Ferry **53** Architect: Mark Becker, Inc. **54** Architect: J. Allen Sayles. Interior design: Sue Kahn **55** Design Group. Interior design: Judith Owens Interiors. Custom home builder: The Owen Companies. Lighting design: Catherine Ng/Lightsmiths **56 (top)** Interior design: Denise Foley Design and David Brewster **57** Architect: Steven Goldstein Architect **58 (left)** Design: Nancy Cowall Cutler **59 (top)** Lighting Design: Randall Whitehead Lighting, Inc. Architect: Erikson Zebroski Design Group **59 (bottom)** Interior design: Greg Mewbourne. Architect: David Gillespie **60** Interior design: Jeanese Rowell Design **61** Interior design: Pamela Pennington/Tsun Yen Tang Wahab/Pamela Pennington Studios **62 (all)** Design: Gordana Pavlovic/Design Studio Gordana LLC **63** Interior design: Renne Prudhomme, Vicki Saxton/Flegels. LCO flat screen television: Sound Perfection. Wall system fabrication: Segale Bros. **64 (top)** Design: Sandra C. Watkins. Paint color and fabrics: Joan Osburn/Osburn Design **64 (bottom)** Interior design: Sandy Crawford. Architect: Steve Feller **65 (top)** Architect: Thomas Bateman Hood **65 (bottom)** Interior design: Molly McGowan Interiors. Cabinetry: Rutt of Lafayette **66** Architect: Mark Becker Inc. **67** Architect: Steven Goldstein **68 (both)** Design: Aleks

Istanbullu Architects **69 (top)** Design: Kent and Pam Greene **69 (bottom)** Architect: Mark Becker Inc. **70** Design: Bret Hancock/Thacher & Thompson Architects **71** Interior design: Barbara Jacobs. Cabinetry fabrication: Dana Karren **72 (top)** Interior design: Lisa Malloy/ Interior Inspirations **72 (bottom)** Architect/designer: Donald Clement. Cabinet fabrication: Apple Woodworks **73 (top)** Architect: Remick Associates Architects-Builders, Inc. **73 (bottom)** Architect: David Trachtenberg Architects **74 (top)** Architect: Gary Earl Parsons **74 (bottom left)** Design: Andre Rothblatt Architecture **74 (bottom right)** Design: Mercedes Corbell Design + Architecture **75 (top)** Architect: Jarvis Architects **75 (bottom)** Architect: Sanborn Designs Incorporated **77** Architect: Luther M. Hintz. Interior design: Pamela Pearce Design **78** Design: Celeste Lewis Architect **79 (bottom left)** Architect: Bassenian/Lagoni Architects. Interior design: Pacific Dimensions, Inc. **79 (bottom right)** Design: Charles Wooldridge **80 (both)** Design: W. David Martin, Architect **83** Studio Becker **84 (top)** Interior design: Lisa Malloy/ Interior Inspirations **85 (top left)**

California Closets **85 (bottom left)** Whirlpool

A SHOPPER'S GUIDE

86 Interior design: Mark Mack **90 (bottom)** Ikea **92 (top left)** Ikea **92 (top right)** Zinc Details **93 (top right)** Studio Becker **94 (upper left)** Studio Becker **94 (upper right)** The Kitchen Source/The Bath & Beyond **94 (bottom left)** Häfele America Co. **94 (bottom right)** Eurodesign Ltd. **99 (top right)** Rev-A-Shelf **99 (bottom right)** Interior design: Kremer Design Group **100 (both)** Fenton MacLaren Home Furnishings **101 (top left)** Design: Debra S. Weiss **101 (bottom left)** Interior design: Barbara Jacobs/Barbara Jacobs Interior Design. Cabinets: Al Orozco **101 (bottom right)** San Anselmo Country Store **102 (both)** Galvins Workspace Furniture **103** Interior design: Claudia Fleury/Claudia's Designs **104 (top)** Ikea **104 (bottom)** Galvins Workspace Furniture **105 (top right)** Ikea **106 (both)** Eurodesign Ltd. **107** House of European Design **109 (bottom left)** Ikea **109 (bottom right)** Eurodesign Ltd. **110** Interior design: Gigi Rogers Design **111 (top all)** Ikea **113 (bottom all)** The Kitchen Source/The Bath

& Beyond **114** Organized Living **115 (top and bottom right)** Organized Living **115 (bottom left)** Ikea **116 (both)** House of European Design **117 (bottom)** Organized Living **118 (center left)** Häfele America Co. **119 (top and bottom left)** Eurodesign Ltd. **119 (bottom right)** Häfele America Co. **120 (top left)** Eurodesign Ltd. **120 (bottom left)** Häfele America Co. **120 (top right)** Interior design: Steven W. Sanborn **121 (top and center right)** Eurodesign Ltd. **121 (bottom left)** Galvins Workspace Furniture

BACK MATTER

126 Architect/designer: Donald Clement. Cabinet fabrication: Apple Woodworks **127** Architect: Edward Buchanan/Jarvis Architects

photography

Jean Allsopp: 25 bottom left, 64 bottom; **Ron Anderson/ Gloria Gale:** 79 top; **Michael Bruk:** 65 top; **Grey Crawford:** 68 all; **Tria Giovan:** 36 bottom, 47 left; **John Granen:** 37; **Ken Gutmaker:** 23 top left, 48 bot-

tom, 74 bottom left, 94 top right, 103; **Jamie Hadley:** 5, 11 top left and right, 12–13 all, 21 bottom left and top three, 22 bottom, 23 bottom left, 24 top right, 25 bottom right, 26, 28 bottom, 29, 33, 40 all, 41, 42 bottom, 43 all, 44 bottom, 45, 47 bottom right, 50 bottom, 53 right, 57, 62 all, 64 top, 66 bottom, 67, 69 bottom, 71, 72 all, 73 bottom, 75 top, 83, 84 top, 88–93 all, 94 left top and bottom, 96–97 all, 99 bottom left, 100 all, 101 bottom right, 102 all, 104–108 all, 109 bottom left and right, 110 bottom, 111 top three, 114 left, 115–117 all, 118 left, 119 top and bottom left and right, 120 left top and bottom, 121–122 all, 124 left and bottom, 125 all, 126, 127; **Philip Harvey:** 25 top right, 32 top, 34 top, 42 top, 49, 50 top, 52, 55, 59 top, 73 top, 74 top, 75 bottom, 77, 94 bottom right, 95, 98, 99 bottom right, 111 bottom, 112–113 all, 119 middle right, 120 right top and bottom; **Alex Hayden:** 69 top, 78; **Muffy Kibbey:** 85 bottom left; **Sylvia Martin:** 59 bottom; **E. Andrew McKinney:** 1, 19, 30 bottom, 31 top left, 38, 46 top, 54 bottom, 56 top, 60 bottom, 63, 65 bottom, 79 bottom left, 101 left top and bottom, 110 top; **Kit Morris:** 47 top, 58 left; **Bradley Olman:** 84 bottom; **Heather Reid:** 74 bottom right; **Tom Rider:** 7; **Mark Rutherford:** 124 top right; **Michael Shopenn:** 79 bottom right; **Michael Skott:** 30 top, 32 bottom left, 34 bottom, 46 bottom, 109 top; **Robin Stancliff:** 39 right; **Thomas J. Story:** 2, 35, 70 bottom, 80 all, 114 right, 118 right top and bottom; **Tim Street-Porter:** 24 bottom left, 81 bottom left, 85 bottom right, 86; **Roger Turk:** 81 top; **Brian Vanden Brink:** 11 top, 21 bottom right, 23 bottom right, 51, 56 bottom, 58 right, 76 bottom, 82 bottom, 101 top right; **Michael Venera/Pottery Barn:** 31 bottom; **David Wakely:** 32 bottom right; **Jessie Walker:** 81 bottom right; **Eric Zepeda:** 61

index

Numbers in **boldfaced type** refer to photographs.